21_{ST}

CENTURY SELLING

SECRETS

ERICA COMBS

ISBN: 0-9740924-4-7

More Heart Than Talent Publishing, Inc.

6507 Pacific Ave #329
Stockton, CA 95207 USA
Toll Free: 800-208-2260
www.MHTPublishing.com

FAX: 209-467-3260

Cover art by FlowMotion Inc.

Printed in the United States of America

Kepi - This book is for you with all my love.
You are my hero. Thank you for setting our sail.

FOREWORD

In 1998, I began my career as a network marketer. I had been in sales for years, so I had a perception that I would transition effortlessly into direct sales and multilevel marketing. After attracting a great deal of rejection and what seemed like an insurmountable wall of transitioning product users to business builders, I knew I required assistance. I was frustrated and started to look for reasons why network marketing wasn't working as opposed to seeking out reasons to validate the growing profession.

Two years later I experienced my very own "annus horriblus," or horrible year. I had been diagnosed with a degenerative disease, gone through a painful divorce, and found myself financially devastated. I was over $100,000 in debt and had lost my house, my health, and my self-esteem. I didn't have a lot of hope. I knew that I had to find something to pull me up, but I wasn't sure what that "something" was.

I had always been great at sales, so I went back to work in the health club industry, sliding into my comfort zone as a manager. Being type A and very aggressive, I easily performed. The secret to my success was that I had always found it effortless to sell to others. I took a $300,000 department to $1 million dollars in just a few months. I was so good at what I was doing that I became bored.

At this time I was reintroduced to network marketing by a client, and I jumped in with both feet. Again I thought that I would be just as successful as I was in my health club job. And again, I was mistaken. This is one of the fundamental rules of business – never become overconfident or complacent. Thankfully, just when I thought about quitting, I was introduced to some audiotapes by Jeff Combs. These would forever shape my future.

Through Jeff, I learned how to qualify people in record time, develop posture, deal with rejection, and attract better people. Jeff is a master trainer. He has the ability to get people to the heart of what holds them back. I have never met anyone like him.

On my journey to becoming a self-made millionaire, I hired Jeff as a coach. It was at this point in my life that I met a dynamic lady who was intelligent, thoughtful, talented, and poised: Jeff's wife Erica. One day Jeff and I were on the phone and he said, "Susan, I want you to meet Erica." Erica and I connected later that day, and I knew that we would be lifelong friends.

Erica and I share much common ground. She comes from a highly successful selling background. In fact, in her industry it was well known that if the deal was going to get done, the job had to be given to Erica. Erica has done it all. She has worked in the hospitality industry and earned her stripes in customer service. When it comes to sales, Erica is one of the most highly skilled, well-rounded people I know.

Erica has also triumphed over personal challenges. These challenges would have left many people struggling to find their place in the world. Erica has risen to new heights, and today she is a self-made millionaire, author, speaker, and trainer, as well as an accomplished athlete.

One thing I would love to share about my friend Erica is that she puts her heart and soul into any project. When I was reading the initial chapters for this book, I was powerfully impacted by Erica's strong desire to assist everyone by telling it like it is and not "sugar coating" the topic. This book will empower anyone to achieve greater skills and confidence in sales. From asking questions to creating a script that works, Erica covers every aspect of selling.

In the 21st century, it is easy to get seduced into Internet marketing and selling at a distance. But regardless of what industry you are in, it is inevitable that you must build relationships to create, build, and maintain your customer base. Selling is a relationship business, and that is why this book may just be one of the most influential pieces you'll ever read.

Sales is the highest paid profession in the world – and, like it or not, we all participate in some form of sales. When we think of sales, we tend to imagine a traditional selling job such as real estate, insurance, or retail. Additionally, every entrepreneur is in sales, because if you cannot sell yourself you will not survive. What we do not tend to realize is that even a stay-at-home mom is a salesperson; she is constantly selling her children on the notion of why they need to get ready for school on time or take a bath. We all sell.

To embrace sales is to enter into a journey. The more people you connect with, the more positive you are, and the more open you become will dictate your success. Success is the person you become in this process, not a paycheck at the end of the journey. Erica talks about how people can fall victim to "entrepreneurial seizure" by thinking so much that they fail to act. In this book, Erica shares the secrets of how to act so you cannot fail if you simply do the work.

Over the course of our seven-year friendship, Jeff and Erica have always given me sage advice. As an entrepreneur, I choose only to mentor with people who are experienced and have been successful in the area that I am in. Erica Combs has encountered and overcome every challenge a person will ever face in sales, and this I why I encourage you to apply the principles, do the exercises, and create the life of your dreams using *21st Century Selling Secrets*.

In health, abundance, and fulfillment,

Susan

Susan Sly is a mother of three beautiful children – Avery, AJ, and Sarai – and loving life partner to her husband Chris. Susan is the author of ***The Have It All Woman***, a practical guide to abundance and fulfillment and coauthor of ***MLM Woman*** – twenty ready-to-use tips for women wanting to create a prosperous network marketing career. Susan is a successful entrepreneur and self-made millionaire.

TABLE OF CONTENTS

21ST
CENTURY SELLING
SECRETS

ERICA COMBS

INTRODUCTION:
THE POWER OF SALES

For decades, sales has provided fodder for many jokes. While humorous, most cast the sales industry in an unsavory light. Like this, for instance:

When a young salesman met his untimely end, he was informed that he had a choice about where he would spend his eternity: heaven or hell. He was allowed to visit both places and then make his decision afterwards.

"I'll see heaven first," said the salesman, and an angel led him through the gates on a private tour. Inside, it was very peaceful and serene, and all the people there were playing harps and eating grapes. It looked very nice, but the salesman was not about to make a decision that could very well condemn him to a life of musical produce.

"Can I see hell now?" he asked. The angel pointed him to the elevator, and he went down to the basement where he was greeted by one of Satan's loyal followers. For the next half hour, the salesman was led on a tour of what appeared to be the best nightclubs he'd ever seen. People were partying loudly and having, if you'll pardon the expression, a hell of a time.

When the tour ended, he was sent back up to the angel, who asked him if he had reached a final decision.

"Yes, I have," he replied. "As great as heaven looks and all, I have to admit that hell was more my kind of place. I've decided to spend my eternity down there."

The salesman was sent to hell, where he was immediately thrown into a cave and chained to a wall and subjected to various tortures. "When I came down here for the tour," he yelled with anger and pain, "I was shown a whole bunch of bars and parties and other great stuff! What happened?"

The devil replied, "Oh, that! That was just the *sales demo.*"

Are you beginning to realize that, regardless of your motivation to join the sales industry, there are many mixed messages and preconceptions about your new career to identify and release? Here are just a few of the disempowering messages most people think of when they hear the word "sales":

Stigma of the used car salesman or vitamin salesman
Great salespeople can sell ice to an Eskimo
Salespeople have the gift of gab
All salespeople care about is money and closing the deal
Salespeople are misleading, dishonest and untrustworthy

Take a moment to list some of your own preconceptions about sales and salespeople:

_____

_____

_____

_____

_____

_____

_____

_____

_____

_____

Now the good news!

Did you know that sales professionals are among the highest paid professionals in the world? Have you ever considered that once you master how to produce within the sales industry, you will have unlimited earning potential for the rest of your life? That's how powerful the sales industry is, and regardless of the company, product, or service that has led you here, you have the opportunity to learn the skills of the trade and create as much revenue as you desire.

What provoked you to explore your own career in sales? Was it the opportunity to achieve limitless wealth, the freedom to set your own hours, your love of people, and the opportunity to connect with them, or were your competitive juices fired when you saw the benefits and rewards of becoming a top producer? Regardless of your motivation, you are now part of one of the most powerful and profitable industries in the world, and while you may feel energized and optimistic about the results you will create, the $7,000,000 question is, "How do I do this?"

First, realize that mastering the game of sales requires lots of experience. The adage of the Natural Born Salesman is completely false. In fact, now that you are in sales, it is time to release this myth and classify the Natural Born Salesman in the same category in your mind as Bigfoot and the Loch Ness Monster. There are many myths surrounding the sales industry and many clichés associated with it. Now that you are in sales, it is time to be proud of your vocation and release any ideas or preconceptions about what it means to be a salesman or saleswoman.

Professional salespeople who achieve great wealth understand the importance of honesty, integrity, and representing themselves and their product properly. They never speak what they cannot deliver. The truly great salesperson knows the power of under promising and over delivering. Most people have a compulsion to over promise and under deliver, leaving their customers feeling let down and dissatisfied. When you under promise and over deliver, you become your customer's hero, and suddenly not only have you served a customer, you have created a lifelong client.

You have a tremendous opportunity as a salesperson to create the life you have always dreamed of through your sales endeavors, and the content of this book is designed to assist you in your transition from amateur to professional!

DEVELOPING A SALES PERSEPECTIVE

Perspective can be defined as your point of view. It's your ability or capacity to view life and situations in their true relationships or relative importance. Why is your perspective so imperative? Why do I feel that perspective is a key to creating success in sales? Let me tell you why, my friends.

How Your History Affects Your Present Reality

Each and every one of us has a past. We have a physical past, we have an emotional past, we have a spiritual past, and each of our relationships has a past. We have a history, and what happens for most of us is that we are so emotional about where we've been that we project those emotions from our past into our future. That creates emotional anxiety, and we worry about what might happen when _____ happens. We worry about the "what ifs" in life: "What if I fail? What if this doesn't work? What if it *does* work? What if my relationships change? What if this isn't what I expected it to be?" In reality, nothing has happened yet. What we end up creating are false realities that we buy into subconsciously, and then that anxiety becomes so consistent in our current method of emotional operation that it actually becomes part of our personality and transforms into our identity.

For those of you who are really committed to understanding why you do what you do, you definitely deserve to experience the movie *What the BLEEP Do We Know!?* In this movie, Dr. Joe Dispenza creates an amazing statement: "You cannot change your reality as long as you're connected to the same identity." He meant that it's not possible to create change until you've changed your old identity. Part of changing your identity is changing your perspective. Changing your perspective on how your history impacts your present is imperative to success in sales, because your results today are a physical manifestation of your historical beliefs. If what you are seeking in your sales career is to create the opportunity to attract a different reality tomorrow than what you experienced today as a result of your history, then that is going to require a shift in your perspective. The great playwright William Shakespeare wrote one line in his play *The Tempest* that absolutely began to change my own emotional perspective. This line is simply, "Your past is merely your prologue."

Many fiction books have a prologue before the body of the story. The prologue is a history of the situation; it sets the scene or relays history of a character that sets the stage to let the reader know where the story begins today.

What if your past – whether it's a fifty-year-old past or a twenty-year-old past or a sixteen-year-old past – what if your past simply became your prologue? What if it were simply a foreshadowing to give someone else an idea of where you've been to know where you're operating from and what's changing so you can begin to rewrite your story each and every day? What if, instead of allowing your history to overshadow where you start operating from at the beginning of each and every day, you could simply brush it off as your prologue, one or two pages of setup, so that you could begin to write the chapter of the volume of your life each and every single day? Wouldn't this be an empowering shift in perspective? What I see far too many of us doing, far too consistently, is being so connected to the identity of who we've been and what we've done or have not done in our past that it sabotages us from creating the results that we desire to manifest in our present.

Your past is your history. In relationships and in life, it really doesn't mean much. It doesn't matter where you've been. What matters is where you are committed to going, the changes you are committed to creating, the leadership skills you are committed to developing, and the impact you are going to create on society – not just through your own personal endeavors, but through your collaboration with the people you attract during your career. In the relative importance, the grand scheme of time, how important is your past really? The answer is that it really isn't important.

Great inventors like Alexander Graham Bell and Thomas Edison are not remembered for their dysfunctions; we don't remember them for all their failed experiments. We remember them for the one situation that they were able to create during their lifetime that impacted society forevermore. It wasn't the failed experiences that brought them fame, it was the experiments that actually returned a result which impacted society forever.

Operate Effectively Within Your Dysfunction

Unless we have previous sales experience, most of us come into this industry experimenting. We feel like we have this blank canvas in front of us; we have our tools, our paints, our brushes, our scripts, and our lead lists, and we're just going to throw paint on that canvas and hope some of it sticks somewhere. That is called an experiment. And yes, this process requires some experimentation to find out how you can operate effectively within your own emotional dysfunction.

"Operate effectively in my dysfunctions? What on earth does this mean?" I'm talking about taking business personally versus professionally. What I mean is that, no matter how professional we all become in business, we're still interrelating on a personal level. Technology cannot make all of our calls for us. Machines and phone trees and automated systems serve a purpose, but at some point we all require that human-to-human personal touch. This requires you to be willing to experiment long enough to discover how to become effective in your interpersonal communications within your own dysfunction. It requires that you begin to shift your perspective about your current reality. Instead of taking every situation as a personal edification of who you are or who you are not, you begin to shift your perspective to become much more objective.

What typically happens is that you take your standard operating procedure with you into your new venture. You take how you've learned to operate within a job to get a paycheck, safely within your own dysfunctions, and you bring those same job skills and that same job mentality with you into sales. You find out very quickly that in sales you're not paid for spinning your wheels. The marketplace doesn't care if you spend 24/7 being busy. All the marketplace is looking for is results, and the more effective you become at creating results within your own identity, whatever that may be, the more results you're going to achieve in a compressed time frame. This is called producing more results with less effort.

Consider this for a moment. If we're all humans with a level of dysfunction, isn't it entirely possible that the people on the other end of your leads list, at the other end of your conversation, at the other end of your interpersonal relationships, is going to be at least as dysfunctional as you?

An Objective vs. Personal Perspective

One Saturday, I went to a Jeep dealership about ninety minutes from where we live in Stockton. I drove my 2005 Jeep with the intention and the decision that I was going to buy a new Jeep Rubicon. I arrived at the dealership at 12:30 in the afternoon, and as it happened, I had to leave by 2:00 to get to another store before they closed. That only left me ninety minutes from the time I walked through the door of the dealership to the time I completed the purchase, which I was already committed to doing. So when my salesman came up and introduced himself to me, I said, "Ben, let me introduce myself. My name is Erica Combs. I can be the easiest lay down sale who ever walked through the doors of your dealership." He said, "How do you know what a lay down sale is?" I said, "Not only do I have years of experience in the sales and marketing industry, I also teach great sales skills. So here's the situation. If you can calculate the numbers correctly on my trade-in versus my new car, I can buy it today. However, if you want to spend a lot of time negotiating a deal and haggling over the numbers, then it's going to require about two weeks for my husband and I to collaborate on a decision and come in together because of my travel schedule. So it's entirely up to you whether you would like to close the sale today or two weeks from now. By the way, I have an appointment and I'm required to leave the dealership exactly at 2:00 pm. Can you talk to whomever you require a conversation with and get this ball rolling?" He said, "Yes, ma'am, absolutely." By 1:45, I'd signed the papers; by 2:00 on the dot, I drove out of the dealership in my new car.

I had a bit of a different experience talking to the gentleman in the service department. In my new Jeep the soft top was installed inside the hard top, and I knew I didn't want the soft top. I've been driving a Jeep for three years, and I've never once used the soft top. When I called the service manager, I said, "Bob, my Jeep is being getting clear-coated and scotch-guarded on Thursday. I'm leaving it there until Saturday. I would like you to dismantle the soft top and leave the hard top installed." He said, "Ma'am, I just did this for an eighteen-year-old girl, and then she was very upset and it cost me two-and-a-half hours of labor, etc." I said, "Bob, precisely what does that situation have to do with this conversation today?"

You see, I had to adjust my perspective and realize that Bob was telling me that he didn't want to do any extra work. I said, "Bob, I can appreciate your previous experience, but I am a woman who knows her own mind, and I know exactly what I want. Here is what I desire and if this is too taxing for you to enter into the computer system, perhaps it would be better to speak to a supervisor within your department who can guarantee that the work will be performed to my expectation between Thursday and Saturday when I pick up my vehicle." All of a sudden, Bob and I developed a whole different level of respect and understanding in our conversation. But it would have been very easy for me to take Bob's position personally, because he assumed he was talking to another young woman on the telephone that wanted one thing and then would change her mind. Instead, it required me to shift my perspective from taking Bob so personally and thus shift the conversation to say, "No, this is professional, this is about what I want, this is about the fact that I deserve to receive what I desire because of this purchase. Bob, if you are not the gentleman to create this situation for me, give me the courtesy of putting me on the phone with the person who can."

Taking it personally and becoming rude, obnoxious, upset, or defensive would not have created the outcome that I was seeking. This is why it's important for you to create some objectivity in your perspective between what is personal and what is professional. Creating results in sales requires that you become objective enough to remain professional even when situations could be interpreted personally. This is one of the main differences between creating prosperity versus merely surviving.

In my opinion, there are two kinds of people in this world: simply average and exceptional. Most people are very happy to settle for being average and merely getting by. Most are willing to settle for having a life somewhere above the mere survival level, having enough so that they are comfortable but not enough to really feel fulfilled by their experience. And there are exceptional people who are not willing to settle for what life would hand them. People like you and me who look at the world and say, "Why not me? Why not now?" Getting past mere survival requires a transition into becoming well-versed and comfortable with prosperity.

Prosperity – Being in the Flow

Prosperity is a word that comes from the Latin word *prospero,* which means "in the flow." Effortless prosperity requires staying in the flow of life, staying within the flow of your service, within the flow of your company. If we could stay in the flow of life more often instead of focusing on the resistance that takes us out of the flow of life, creating the results that we seek and desire would be much easier.

Success in sales is really about letting go of control; it's about letting go of personal attachments, it's about letting go of taking life so personally. It's about letting go of every situation that's an edification of either who you haven't yet become or how you haven't grown yet. It's realizing that no matter how good any of us get, we'll still meet with some resistance on our own journey. This is just part of life; it's being a soul, having a human experience. An existence where there is no resistance, where all is effortless prosperity, is called utopian for a very good reason. Between theory and fantasy you will find reality. It's where the reality of your emotions and the information and technology of the world finds you, despite your best intentions to unplug and walk on a path of ease. Continuing to walk that path of ease towards your prosperity requires that you remain focused on your reason why, focused on why you're unplugging, and focused on why you are operating differently from the status quo.

Creating a Million Millionaires

For instance, if you decide, as Jeff and I have, not to partake in all the negative news that sells newspapers and keeps radio stations and television stations in business across the globe, you will find that people are incredulous that you have no consciousness of all the bad things that are happening globally in our economy or locally in our society. And yet, I have found that in creating peace in my own life and in the lives of those I'm able to impact through my energetic reach, staying connected to all of the bad things that are happening worldwide does not serve me to raise my energy frequencies to a level where more people are attracted to me and connected to my message. I have learned that the more people are attracted to my message, the more effortlessly I can impact the masses. Within the masses I'm finding the classes who are willing to go through some of the same transformations emotionally and personally that I have gone through in order to collaborate with me to bring the message to even more people. Imagine what would happen if those million people became so focused on their prosperity consciousness that together we created a million millionaires. A million millionaires would have a whole different level of leverage in order to create change and create results within today's society, because they would be able to lead with their wallets, not just their ideas.

Operating as if Money Wasn't an Issue

It's said that money talks and ideas walk. While it doesn't always require money to find a voice, money buys options, and money does gain attention. Money creates prosperity, where you can operate when money is no longer an issue. Are you tired of being limited by your bank account balance? Are you tired of being limited by the credit card bills you cannot pay? In order to release that limitation, in order to operate as if money weren't an issue, you have to begin by operating without money being an issue. This doesn't mean that you become compulsively consumptive in your habits. It does mean that you begin to operate by creating investments in your own awareness, in your own physical reality, and in your own consciousness. It's not about spending frivolously, but about investing wisely.

It means investing wisely in something as trivial as replacement razor blades in your shaver to something as imperative as the nutrition that you purchase for your family and how you plan your meals. When you begin operating as if money was not an issue, it may mean consuming less food but consuming a higher quality food. You may sacrifice quantity for quality, but is that really a sacrifice?

I'll never forget a conversation that Jeffrey had with Burke Hedges who wrote the best-selling book *Who Stole the American Dream?* Jeff said, "Burke, baby, I'm just paying the price," and Burke said, "Jeff, it is not a price. What you and I and Erica have a chance to do each and every day is an absolute privilege." That one statement started to change our perspective on the industry. Sure, it can seem like a grind at times, but we have to understand that it's the idea that it's painful, the resistance that holds us back, that takes us out of focus. It's this idea that the process is slow, that you're not getting anywhere, that you haven't made any progress, that no one's listening to you, that what you're doing is not important. This is what distracts us from our long-term objective of the change we are seeking to create.

Desiring More

Desiring *more* is the reason we come into this game. It may be more time, more money, more freedom, or the opportunity to choose what you do while you're living rather than just do what you can to make a living. It can just be the option of deciding how you spend your time in the time that you exist in on this planet. Whatever "more" means to you, whatever the reason you came to free enterprise, if you are like most of us, you will discover a bigger sense of purpose at some point on your journey. You don't have to know what it is today.

Discovering a Deeper Purpose

I entered free enterprise back in the year 2000 looking for more. I wanted a way to create freedom in my life: financial freedom, emotional freedom, resiliency, freedom to travel, freedom to produce, freedom to dictate, freedom to just have the opportunity to command the universe to provide what I deserve as a return on my energy. I wanted to be my own unique marketing proposition. It was within this context that in 2003 I said, "Wow, this is great. I'm finally living my dreams, but what is it that I want to do? What's bigger than me? What's more than what I'm already creating?"

That's when I created my *Women in Power* website. Eighty

percent of our industry is made up of women, yet I could not find any material on how to succeed as a woman in free enterprise. I realized that there was obviously a niche that had not been filled. I thought, "Why don't I create it? Why don't I create a forum for entrepreneurial women worldwide to be able to connect and collaborate – an online forum that's completely generic where women can share their stories, post their issues, upload a picture, discuss what they're doing, why they're in free enterprise, what challenges they may be experiencing, and what triumphs they've been creating?" I felt a passion and a driving inspiration to create a symposium for women to connect and create the kind of sisterhood that everyone talks about and no one has ever actually put into place. I've been doing this step-by-step, little by little, on a daily basis since that epiphany in October 2003.

Your objective may simply be more money for you and your family now, or perhaps it's being able to have more options. Money doesn't make the world go round, love does, but money definitely pays for the trip. Money is what is going to allow you to create options to design the reality that you seek, rather than settling for the circumstances that life would otherwise hand to you. And it's not just life; it's also society. Let's say you present your case to society: "Here's my history, here's my family, here's what I've been through.... What do I deserve?" Society is pretty much going to hand you the exact situation you are seeking to release through your entrepreneurial endeavor.

Raising Society's Consciousness

There is a whole new wave of personal development starting to create change right now through movies like *What the BLEEP* and *The Secret*. These movies teach us about our intrinsic spiritual value; they assist us to understand that we deserve prosperity in abundance, because we exist, and because abundance is a natural state within the universe. This information is absolutely true, and it's beginning to raise the consciousness of our society as a whole. It is starting to shift our society's perspective one person at a time. It's very powerful when you can start to impact thousands and then millions of people through a message, not just because of your own marketing endeavors, but because of the energy that it picks up. The movie *Pay It Forward* is the epitome of direct selling, network marketing, and practical experience. This is about someone being impacted by you to such an extent that they feel emotionally compelled to share the message with someone else. This is how any business endeavor starts to gain momentum.

If you are not experiencing momentum in your career today, it's time to change your perspective about your enterprise. Now is the time to shift your focus back to revenue-producing activity. The paperwork shuffling is over, my friends. The number crunching is done. Let it go, let it be. DFC – Done, Finished, Completed. Now is the time to create results, results that will lead you to that land of personal freedom you have been seeking. Do you realize that you can create anywhere from two to six sales a week, depending on the amount of time you have to dedicate to your career and the level of urgency you feel to create results? What this is going to require is a connection back to your cerebral cortex and a release of your limbic system.

Understanding How Your Brain Works

Here's how this works. The cerebral cortex is the frontal portion of your brain. Your cerebral cortex is where your higher consciousness happens. This is where your intellectual thinking occurs, where your emotions occur, and where the connections between events and how you feel occur. Your higher level of consciousness is all in the frontal region of your brain where your forehead and your hairline meet.

The limbic system is a small, walnut-sized portion of your brain that exists exactly where the top of your neck meets the base of your skull. Your limbic system is your flight or flight survival mechanism. The whole purpose of your limbic system is merely to survive. Every single mammal and reptile that lives on the globe has a limbic system. It is the primal survival mechanism of any living organism with a brain. The whole purpose of survival is procreation – surviving long enough to procreate to ensure the continuation of that particular species. It's simply there to propel our bodies to survive the environmental factors that we are experiencing in order to live another day.

What happens is that we are conditioned by our environmental factors to spend far too much time living in survival mode, living to live another day, living to wake up another morning, even though we are dissatisfied with our current reality. We get so distracted from our higher focus, the reason we are seeking change, the philanthropic causes, the charities that we would make donations to, the organizations we would set up to create change, all of the higher reasons of consciousness that lead us to free enterprise. We get caught in our limbic system, and we get distracted from the positive thought patterns that lead us to believe that we could change our current reality based on our own entrepreneurial experience.

Your Thoughts Are Real

Our thoughts are real. The thoughts we think each day create a biochemical response within our brain. We have a thought, and as a result our brain releases chemicals. An electrical transmission occurs through the synapses between the nerve endings in our brain, and we become aware of what we have thought. We think the thought, our brain fires, it releases chemicals, and then we become aware of the thought that we've already created. What this means is that our bodies have reacted physically before we're even conscious and aware of the thought that has triggered this biological response within our bodies. So when you have the thought, "Oh my God, this bill is coming; how am I going to pay it?" that thought has already created a chemical release of anxiety which triggers the fight or flight response within your limbic system. You're already feeling threatened before you've even acknowledged the thought that led you to release the chemicals in your brain that said, "I'm not safe," to the rest of your body. Your limbic system responds by releasing adrenaline into your body, and so your pulse increases, your rate of respiration increases, and you're ready to respond to a threat that hasn't even happened yet. If you were out in the wild, fighting for existence against threatening predators, you might have an encounter with a lion. The lion would chase you, your fight or flight response would pick up, and you would run from the lion. Hopefully you would escape, and then the lion that chased you would stop and rest, and you, after escaping the attack, would rest too. It's in that resting phase that your body can release and break down and disseminate all those hormones and chemicals like adrenaline and cortisol that occur because of this response to stress.

Becoming Aware of How Your Thoughts Affect You

But in today's society, we are constantly bombarded by stress. You are constantly bombarded with messages and signals, and a lot of them trigger an emotional reaction from you. Often it's a reaction you're not even aware of until your body has already responded based on a chemical reaction that happened in your brain. Suddenly you become consciousness of the thought that you can't pay your bills, and your body begins reacting to not having the money before you're even in the situation of not having the money. Conversely, you're involved in the exact opportunities that could allow you to create the money ahead of time. It is a mind-boggling mess when you start to break it down and understand the psychoses and the psychology behind this whole idea of creation, behind this whole existence that we get so enmeshed and so wrapped up in. Part of what is required to change this operation is an understanding that your thoughts release brain chemicals that create an electrical transmission across your brain where it causes you to become aware of what you've thought. You must understand that your thoughts are real, and they have a real impact on how you feel and how you behave.

Beginning to notice how negative thoughts affect your body. Notice how your body responds to anger, how it responds to unkind thoughts, sad thoughts, or cranky thoughts. Every time you have negative thoughts, your brain releases chemicals that make your body feel bad, thus activating your limbic system. When your body feels bad, it goes into a fight or flight response. Think about the last time you were angry. How did your body feel? If you are like most people, your muscles tense up, your heart beats faster, and your hands start to sweat. Sometimes you may even feel a little bit dizzy. What is interesting is that you respond physiologically the same way whether you're actually feeling angry or just perceiving that you feel angry.

When athletes have been hooked up to EKG devices to measure the way their muscle and nerve endings respond when they are physically engaging in their athletic competitions. Next they watch videos in which they are transposed into a virtual reality situation where it seems as if they are actually competing in an event. Their muscles, neurons, and nerve cells are activated just as if they were actually physically doing the exercise. This proves that our brains command our bodies. It means that what we focus on grows. It means

33

that *perceived* pain and *felt* pain create exactly the same physical and emotional responses within the physical cells of our body. So it is no wonder that if we have been conditioned to struggle our entire life, when we get put in a position where success is imminent and prosperity is right around the corner, we subconsciously create sabotages to take us back into struggle because that is the condition we have become addicted to operating within. Begin to notice how your body reacts to every thought that you have.

Polygraphs and lie detector tests show us that our bodies react to our thoughts. During a lie detector test, a person is hooked up to equipment that measures hand temperature, heart rate, blood pressure, respiration, muscle tension, and how much perspiration is present on the hands. When the tester asks questions like, "Did you steal that car?" if the person did steal the car, his body will exhibit a stress response which will invoke the machine to read a frequency differently than if he is telling the truth. The subject's hands might get cold or their heart might beat faster; their blood pressure and respiration increases, their muscles gets tight, or their hands begin to sweat. Some reaction takes place physiologically almost immediately that causes the polygraph machine to read the results a little bit differently.

On the other hand, consider a situation that provokes a relaxation response, such as travel to the island destination of your choice or possessing a millionaire's budget. When someone else is paying for an all expense trip where every single requirement that you may have is met, you are waited on hand and foot, and you have no obligation other than to simply relax and enjoy the serenity of your surroundings, that's going to trigger an entirely different physiological response than thinking about what it would feel like to call fifty people who all say no.

Take Control of Your Thoughts by Operating Out of Your Higher Awareness

What's interesting is that most people will never say no to us in a situation where we are seeking a decision on the telephone. Our society is conditioned to expect a certain number of excuses or objections as turnoff valves. When someone says, "I don't have time," you all too often say, "Sorry to bother you." If they say, "I don't have money," you respond with, "I know exactly how that feels; let me let you go," When someone says, "I need to think about it," you say, "Sure, let me call you in three weeks." In other words, you accept excuses as conversation stoppers, when what is really imperative is that you understand that your automatic thoughts and the automatic thoughts of other people do not always tell the truth. You operate far too frequently out of automatic knee-jerk emotional and physiological responses that have nothing to do with the truth. Unless you think about your thoughts, they're automatic, they just happen. But your thoughts don't always tell the whole truth and sometimes your thoughts even lie to you.

I remember at one point in my educational career I thought I was intellectually challenged because I couldn't pass a math course. When I first took Algebra II, I couldn't get through the first semester and my professor failed me because I couldn't pass the test due to my test anxiety. I was already worried about failing before I even sat down to take the test. How many of you do this when it comes to conversing about someone about a business opportunity? You perceive that you are going to fail before you've even had the dialogue. Because you are thinking about what what they're going to ask that you can't answer, you end up getting exactly what you expect. What you can do to start operating more out of your higher consciousness and less out of your limbic system is to begin to change your negative thought patterns. The way you do this is to first become aware of when the very first negative thought enters your mind. If you could start to increase the time lapse from when you think a thought to when you become aware of a thought, it would be much easier to begin to neutralize the thought before it's even created.

What happened for me is that I went back to Algebra I, a class I had already aced. I had been advanced – I was a year ahead of myself in Algebra II. I decided that I would rather repeat a year of Algebra I, knowing that I already understood the information. I chose to receive the results I expected instead of spending another year beating my head against the wall, getting failing grades in a class that I just didn't understand yet. I went back and maintained a 4.0 status in Algebra I. The following year, I took Algebra II from a different professor, and I had an entirely different experience, because I'd been able to go back and recreate that belief system that said, "Tests are easy, I know the answers, passing is effortless."

What If It Was Easy?

What if prospecting could become easy? What if closing sales could become easy? What if knowing the right questions to ask was easy? What if you knew that any time you received the objection, "I don't have the time," you were able to say, "How does it feel not have the time to pursue your dreams?" What if you could learn to use their words in your response and end it with a great question?

For instance, "This sounds great, but I don't have the money." This is a very interesting objection. If it sounded so great, wouldn't they create the money to take advantage of it? Knowing that people buy based on value, if you can assist them to see the value in the opportunity, then it's much more likely that they're going to buy. What if you said, "I can appreciate your position, but do you see the value in what this experience could create for you and your family?"

When you learn to use your prospect's words and create your response in the form of a question, you start to take them back to the frontal region of their brain. All of the excuses people give you about why they can't buy are a survival response. Survival is why they feel that they have to hang on to their money. It's why they have to continue to struggle. They're not realizing that in a state of higher consciousness they could get involved in an opportunity that could create so much wealth that bills don't matter.

Recently I was in Medford, Oregon, and I was deciding what time I would have to get picked up to take a 6:00 a.m. flight to get back to San Francisco. I said, "I require a 4:00 a.m. pickup at the hotel so I can be in line waiting for the gate to open at 4:15." My contact in Oregon reacted by saying, "4:00 a.m., oh my goodness!" I said, "Well, if that's too early for you, I'll call a taxi company and create arrangements for a taxi to take me to the airport at the exact time I require delivery." He said, "You have no idea how expensive taxies are in Medford!" and I replied, "No, I don't, but what I have found is that expense is all relative to income." That cab fare from the hotel to the airport was $10, but it ended up being $50 because I gave the driver a $40 tip for that service at 4:00 a.m. on a Friday morning. Once again, this is an example of survival versus higher awareness.

Create a New Belief System

In the course of your next week in sales, here are some thoughts to feed your higher consciousness:

1. There are at least two people in this world you would die for.

2. At least fifteen people in this world love you in some capacity.

3. The only reason anyone would ever hate you is because they want to be just like you.

4. A smile from you can bring happiness to anyone, even if they don't like you.

5. Every night someone thinks about you before they go to sleep.

6. You mean the world to someone.

7. You are special and unique.

8. Someone you don't even know exists loves you.

9. Even when you make the biggest mistake, something good comes from it, provided you are in a position to receive the good

10. When you think the world has turned its back on you, take another look – because that's often when you are presented with a new opportunity to grow and change.

11. Always remember and receive the compliments that are extended to you each and every day.

I guarantee for every struggle, for every hardship that you buy into as an excuse "not to," there are at least 11 million people out there who would be grateful to turn in their current circumstances in order to live your experience.

SELF-ESTEEM IN SALES

Self-acceptance and self-esteem are two very powerful experiences you can begin to create for yourself right now in this moment. Each could be a book in and of itself, and indeed, many books have been written to assist people to improve their self-esteem. I am linking them together in this chapter because I have discovered through my own growth that self-acceptance is the foundation for creating a great self-esteem.

Defining Self-Esteem

Self-esteem is not to be confused with self-confidence. Self-confidence is how capable you feel in a situation. It is very easy to feel confident about your ability to perform in a job if this is what you have been doing for most of your life. But now here you are, a professional sales person, and if this is new to you, you may find that your foundation of self-confidence is beginning to wobble if you have not also developed a strong sense of self-esteem.

Self-esteem is how you feel about you, and self-acceptance is the ability to approve of every aspect of yourself as a whole, understanding that as a human being you are in a constant process of growth and transition. Consider for a moment your role models for self-esteem. As a child, did you grow up in a family that fostered a great sense of self for each family member? If your family was dysfunctional, you are in great company! Most people have not come from a healthy, functional family, and each and every one of us carries beliefs and doubts about ourselves based on our childhood experiences. Unless at some point in time you were fortunate enough to have people in your life who accepted and felt good about themselves who you could mentor with and model yourself after, it can be very challenging as an adult to create a great self-esteem.

Self-Esteem: A Critical Ingredient for Success in Sales

Developing a great self-esteem is critical to success in sales. As a salesperson, your prospects buy your uniqueness and energetic value in addition to the products and services you represent. After all, if you do not feel good about yourself, it is very challenging to market your uniqueness and value if you are not able to recognize it. Recognizing your value begins with accepting yourself fully exactly as you are today. It is so easy to get caught up in the idea of "When _____ changes, I will feel good about myself." The paradox is that until you accept where you are in life physically and where you are in your internal growth emotionally, even when you achieve what you desire you will still feel the same way about yourself. Self-acceptance does not mean that you stagnate in your personal or business growth. It means that you begin to view your progress and current situation more objectively (without judgment), realizing that no matter how much you grow, you will always have areas where you seek development. This is why success is a process, not a destination, and the key to this game is to feel good about where you are and who you are becoming on your journey.

not required in order to create results. This requires at some point really letting go of the control of yourself, control of your business, and control of your emotions to establish a command. Letting go of control is realizing that your commodity is people. A people business, by definition, is an imperfect commodity. It means that you have a commodity, which is at least, if not more so, dysfunctional than you are. It should be a huge release for you, a huge breath of fresh air, to realize that "You can't say the wrong thing to the right person." It's not about becoming perfect within your enterprise, but becoming effective within your own dysfunction in your enterprise.

For me, becoming effective within my own dysfunction has meant understanding what makes my emotional clock tick, and what also causes it to stop and have my emotional alarm clock go off. It means really understanding what people, what personalities, and what kind of energy from the present trigger emotions connected to past events, and why that happens. The people in my present reality who trigger my emotions are connected to people in my past reality. I have a lot of experience in my past reality as far as humans and emotions and dysfunctional relationships go. I don't regret a single moment of the life I have led, because it's allowed me to gain a lot of experience and insight and wisdom into who I am, why I do what I do, and why I feel how I feel, the way I respond to certain people in a situation, and certain energies and intensities I experience. And it's my own insight into myself that allows me to have so much insight into the people whom I assist.

This is exactly what can lead you to create a fortune – that goldmine you are seeking through your own business – whatever your reasons are and whatever you intend to do with the money you create as an individual. Success is like the famous saying, "Beauty is in the eye of the beholder." Since your success is only measured by yourself, it's imperative that you allow yourself to begin to understand what makes you tick and what stops your clock. What allows you to be in production, and what takes you out of production? The more you understand and know about yourself, the more you are going to understand, know, and be able to assist the people that you partner with: your clients, your associates, your downline, crossline, bottom line, upline, etc. This kind of connection requires that you release your own internal pressure for perfection.

Letting Go of Perfection

All of us, at some stage in our lives, get conditioned to perform for approval. But now, the only approval you require in order to succeed is your own. You may still desire and seek the approval of your family, friends, and the people who are close to you. But realize that you don't require their acknowledgment, their acquiescence, and their conceptualization of what you're doing in your business in order for you to create results. The only permission you require to be successful is your own.

That means that if you are seeking success within the next twelve months, you'd better get used to not being perfect in order to create that success.If you are requiring perfection from yourself, your emotions, your conversations, your team, and your production, the gauntlet that you're creating based on this idea of perfection is so overwhelming and so rigid, there's no way you could possibly succeed. Success requires your ability to let go.

You'll find on your own journey that the more you're able to release the situations that do not serve you, the more open and available you'll be to attract new people and new situations which do serve you. This is a very contradictory concept to wrap your mind and heart around. Success is not about commanding and controlling; success is about letting go. It's about learning to live a life with ease.

It's about learning to delegate.

If you're like me – an obsessive-compulsive person with control issues – then letting go and delegating are going to be key challenges for you to overcome in order to create success. If you have a six-figure or seven-figure annual objective of what you will create in your enterprise, you are going to require people other than yourself to be involved in order to create those kind of results, and that means learning how to delegate and how to communicate.

It really means learning how to let go of control in order to operate in the middle, to stay in the flow of your enterprise. In order to assist you in learning this, I've come up with seven beliefs that hold you back. We'll cover seven situations that the fledgling, intermediate, or even advanced salesperson buys into that keeps them stuck at the same level of revenue, as well as the ways to neutralize this self-talk and create release and freedom to attract new and different results into your business.

Belief #1: "It's Who You Know"

Everyone says, "It's who you know," but it's not who you know. The truth is it's what you *do* with who you know. Who you know is nothing; what you do with who you know is everything. This is the action that brings success.

For example, I've had the opportunity through our seminar company to meet and collaborate with Mark Victor Hansen and Jim Rohn. Because of the relationship that we established with them, when I wrote *Women in Power: A Woman's Guide to Free Enterprise*, I decided that it would be a very effective and valuable situation to ask both Mark Victor Hansen and Jim Rohn for their endorsements to place on the back cover for sales and marketing purposes.

And because I knew both of them, I put together a letter of introduction and attached the first three chapters of my book and sent them off to Jim Rohn and Mark Victor Hansen's offices, asking if it would be possible if they saw value in my information to send me a testimony or an endorsement within six weeks. My editor hadn't even seen these chapters. They hadn't been proofread; they were full of typos. I didn't even know what my chapter titles for the book were going to be. But I sent them off anyway, and within twenty-four hours I had both of their endorsements! This was a case of who I knew and what I could receive from who I knew. But more importantly, it's about what I did with who I knew that created results. What I did with who I knew put their endorsements on the back cover of my book.

The only challenge was that after I received those endorsements, I couldn't write another page of my book for about six months. Nothing seemed to make sense. I was worried about creating enough value in my book, enough value in my content, to live up to those endorsements. Then Jeff, my great coach, stepped in and said, "Erica, it's time for you to finish this book." And I realized that Mark Victor Hansen and Jim Rohn had written those endorsements based on the value they already perceived that I had the ability to deliver to the marketplace.

So, because they endorsed me, there was actually no way that I could ever disappoint them through anything I wrote after that endorsement. As I was going through this process, as I was stagnating and stuck in my writing, it was challenging for me to realize what was really happening, because at first I didn't understand that I was performing for approval once again. I didn't realize that I was attempting to be so perfect, so neurotic in my perfection, that I was procrastinating. I was actually stifling my own internal voice, not allowing myself to resonate, to deliver my message, to speak to the universe, to attract the people to me who unequivocally deserved my message and would receive value from it. But once I became aware of this, all of it changed really, really fast.

If you're stuck in your enterprise, now is the time for you to make a list of those individuals you know who have influence and affluence, those you haven't talked to yet about your business, those you haven't followed up with, and those you know whose endorsement of your ability as a business person would carry some leverage for you to be able to market yourself more effectively.

Who you know really doesn't mean anything if you never pick up the phone, reach out, and touch someone. Stay connected with the people that you know will support you in your endeavors. Remember, as you become more successful, you also become a bigger target. The more successful you become, the more prosperous you become, the more you will contradict people's identities just based on who you are and what you are doing. Typically, it does you no good to fish for approval in the friends and family pond. This doesn't mean your family and friends don't love you, but their ability to really grasp what you are doing through your sales career is going to be inhibited based on their own beliefs, experiences, the people they do or don't know, and the people they do or don't turn to for insight. If success is what you seek, it becomes your responsibility to acknowledge who you know and how you can leverage yourself to create results through these individuals. This is how all entrepreneurs really start to transform their businesses. It's all about what you do with who you know, how you collaborate with these individuals, what ideas you have, and the courage you have to bring those ideas to the marketplace.

Belief #2: "There's Something Wrong with Me"

The second belief that most of us buy into is also related to the perfection that keeps us stuck. It's the feeling of, "There's something wrong with me." It's a belief that there's something wrong with who you are. It's saying, "I am a failure," rather than saying, "I have challenges in this situation." This can look like a sad form of self-acceptance. In fact, we can even associate such exaggeration with being truthful. "Why not admit it? I'm a failure." However, the statement, "I'm a failure," is a *lie,* and the lie is intentional. The payoff to this lie is, "If I'm already a failure, how can I be criticized for not doing something great?"

The consequences of this kind of self-deception are huge. Buying into the idea that you are a failure because an idea or a strategy didn't pan out the way you expected it to is just one more excuse to legitimize not capitalizing on your brilliance. It's a situation that you create where you are actually contributing to the inhibitions that keep you from succeeding. This is when you take innocent, meaningless situations and add them to your own devastation – you add them to your own meaning of why something is wrong with you. By doing this, you turn situations and experiences into indictments against yourselves. The sum of these unnecessary indictments cause you to believe that you are defective, thus killing your spirit.

This used to happen to me regarding my weight and my body image. I used to tell myself, "There's something wrong with me because my body isn't consistent. There's something wrong with me because I can work out and go to two or three gym classes a day and not lose any weight. There's something wrong with me that I'm more dietary conscious and more conscious of moving my body every day than anyone I know, and yet nothing ever changes." This kind of self-talk kept me out of action. It removed all sense of purpose.

It became a lie that my soul unconsciously absorbed. There was a voice inside of me that said, "It's not safe to live on purpose." This voice said, "It's not safe to express yourself completely in living your true life."

This is the reason that success is too big of an adventure for someone who perceives they have something wrong with them. Success is too big a risk for a defective person to take. But you have to realize that this is the voice of a lie. It's the part of your ego that leads you astray. It's the voice that keeps you from doing exactly what you know is required to create the changes you seek. It's the voice of anxiety and passivity. The opposite of soul purpose is soul surrender. This is an internal defeat. It means quitting before you ever really begin. But recognize that this is also your opportunity to reinvent yourself over and over again to get where you would like to be in your results and in your life.

Recently, Keith, the newest associate in our company, asked me when the next half marathon in our area would be. When I told him, he said, "That's great. Can you create a training program for me so that I can be in condition to run that half marathon?" I said, "Absolutely!"

The half marathon was in October, seventeen weeks away. Now, this year I have had the opportunity to watch my speaking career, my creative career, and my products absolutely bloom and flourish, but that flourishing also created a convenient excuse that there was no way I could train to be a runner and do all of this in our business at the same time. But when Keith asked me for assistance in training for the half marathon, I realized that I absolutely did have time in my schedule for physical training. And so I started to retrain for that event.

I actually ran two half marathons that October. That's 13.1 miles each. This required me to let go of the idea that there was something wrong with me. The challenge was within my own system. The challenge was my all-or-nothing predominance. The challenge was perceiving myself as not good enough because I wasn't running at all, and then wanting to do it all and train for four hours a day. The challenge was finding some middle ground. The truth here is that I required a letting go of control of my life in order to establish a new level of command within the middle. This required that I let go of control in order to create a new action plan in order to achieve the results that I desired. It required courage to hang in there in the middle, acknowledging what served me and what didn't, and acknowledging where I could improve vs. what was outside of my control.

There's always a market for courage. Courage never goes out of style. The truth is, no one is a failure. All people fail at certain things, but no one is a failure. To say someone is a failure is as superstitious as calling that same person a witch or a demon. It's a form of internal fear turned into an external label. You may have had challenges doing some things. You may have had failures in some situations, but there's nothing wrong with you. *You* are not defective. Once you learn to hold onto this truth, it will start to give you your life back.

Belief #3: "I'm Too Old for That"

One of the easiest ways to avoid doing something is to say you are too old to do it. This is a claim that keeps you out of action and sabotages your dreams, although in reality it's almost never really true that you're too old to do what you say you're too old to do. How long ago were you telling yourself you were too young to do things? That you didn't really know how to do that yet, that you didn't have enough experience our confidence? It's amazing how often I hear people in their thirties say, "I'm too old for that." It's their excuse. It's their way out of things. But it's almost never the truth. It's almost always just a feeling covered by an invented fact.

So here's the question: should you honor and respect that feeling, or is it just a familiar old useful feeling that buys you time to get out of doing something where you have some anxiety about the outcome? You have to realize that at some point in life you're going to be confronted with questions like "Is it too late for me to live my dreams? Is it too late for me to produce the results that I desire? What if I'm too old to start a career as a professional salesperson? What if I'm too old to be an entrepreneur?"

Here's the reality: only you can decide if you're too old to do something. Only you can decide if you're too old to change. Only you can decide if you're too old to prosper, and if you decide that you're too old, then you are too old. But the beauty of exposing these beliefs is that it frees you up to live on purpose. These beliefs, these lies, burden the soul; a person with a burdened soul lives randomly. If you want to live on purpose, rather than in random self-deceit, it's going to require that you start understanding that some of the beliefs that you've been buying into are not serving you.

Some of your beliefs require releasing in order for you to move to the next level. I can't tell you how many people have told me they always wanted to be a writer, an actor, or a musician. But now, of course, it's a little late because they are thirty, forty, fifty, or sixty. They say, "I'm too old for that," with a completely straight physical and emotional face. Lying about age is done to hide what is true about action.

time. When the desire is strong enough to create a result, we have all the time in the world in order to put that plan into action.

Jeff and I just looked at a commercial building today. It's not about time, and it's not about money. It's really about deciding that this is the building for us, and that this is what we are going to do. It's deciding that this is how we are going to expand our enterprise. Here is how we are going to align ourselves with our assets – the time we have, the production and results we currently have – and create space to expand our portfolio. To create space to expand the amount of time that we have to enjoy our lives while we're living, not just doing what we do for a living.

You have to realize that when you lie about time, you become an enemy of time. Time starts to run against you and there's never enough. But when you forget time and focus on one situation, one solution, time suddenly is on your side again. It becomes your ally. When time is on your side, this is where life is created. This is where memories happen. This is where uniqueness is created. This is where you have time with your family, time with your friends. Time can always be created, provided you are not using time as an excuse to destroy your reasons to succeed.

Belief #6: "There Is Nothing I Can Do"

What a disempowering belief to maintain and carry with you! Did you ever wake up with the idea that maybe your spirit was fired up on its own, or maybe a movie, a good book, or an inspirational CD or conversation would fire you up? But then the financial, familial, or professional circumstances that you'd been ignoring for long enough pushed you into various corners so that you finally just have to acknowledge and fight your way out of them. Soon the crises have you fired up, and then it becomes a habit. To find energy, you start subconsciously waiting for the crises to get big enough to merit enough information and energy on your part to actually address them. Before the crises hit, when you think about a challenge in any area of your life, you say, "There's nothing I can do." By saying this, you convince yourself you don't have to think any further about the situation you are facing.

The way to neutralize this is to realize that you have absolute command over your life. You don't have to wait for external pressure to force you into action. You can respond to a situation without external pressure or internal guilt in order to create the results that you desire instead of spending quality time unwinding the results that you don't want to have. Saying, "There's nothing I can do," relinquishes all responsibility for the situation that you are facing. Realize instead that if you attract to yourself exactly what you are experiencing, if you attract to yourself situations to edify your places in life, then you also attract to yourself situations that you can grow through, progress through, learn from, and gain insight and knowledge with.

Learn to never walk away defeated from any challenge or situation in life, realizing instead that there is always something you can do to create a result. There's always something you can do to create insight. There's always something you can do to relieve pressure, to create space, to be more in the flow, to be more in the present, to let go of yesterday, and not worry about tomorrow. There's always something you can do in every moment of every phase of every experience of your entire lifetime to choose to be a victor rather than to be a victim.

Belief # 7: "I Worry Because I Care"

What this actually means is that you worry about people so that you can be a victim. You worry about people who are always negative, or those you perceive cannot make it without you. You worry about people that you can rescue, those you can save, massage, coach, and give insight to who will suck your energy but never create any action to change.

When someone asks you why these situations matter to you, you will declare, "It's because I care." You worry because you care about what happens to her, or what happens to him, or what happens to them. You worry that they'll take it wrong if you suggest anything that requires change. You worry they'll take it wrong if you bring them to any kind of support group. You worry that your success could contradict their struggle, and what if your relationship changes?

You worry that if you become more successful than your parents, you won't have a relationship left. You worry that if you disagree, there will never be any middle ground again. But in reality, you don't worry about people because you care about them. You worry because worrying is what you do all day to avoid taking action. You're in the habit of worrying. That's how you occupy your mind. It's become an activity that you can't release from your brain. It's like songs that get on the jingle-track of your brain and you can't get them out of your mind for days. Worrying becomes part of your theme song.

You worry because you don't have any action you can take to fix someone else's problems. And then you worry that you don't have a life of your own, at least not in the sense that your life is intriguing and exciting enough to make other people's habits and challenges not such a big deal. If you had a life of your own, you would not be worried about other people living up to your expectations. If something is missing in them, and you found an opportunity to contribute, you might be in action, but you wouldn't be worrying.

Worrying will not work. For the next two weeks, take immediate notice of every time you worry. When you catch yourself worrying, create an action – any action – just make sure you create one. Do something. Anything – kick a pebble to the other side of the street. Change a coin to the other side of your pocket. Move money around in your billfold. Do something about some situation you have command over, and give yourself permission not to worry about situations that you cannot possibly affect.

This is a great way to train yourself not to worry, especially if you resist being in action. The truth is not, "I worry because I care." The truth is, "I worry because I am in the habit of worrying. I worry in order to do nothing." Doing nothing about a problem soon becomes the problem. The great hockey player, Wayne Gretzky, said, "You miss 100% of the shots that you don't take." This means that the anxiety you have, the worry about the action you might take that doesn't pan out, that doesn't reward you the way you expected it to, the people that don't show up, the way you practiced your speech and yet no one buys from you – all of this anxiety, all of this worry, is so overrated. You're going to hear me say this over and over again: perfection is completely overrated.

People don't care how much you know. They don't care about how perfectly you present your opportunity. They don't care about how perfectly you explain the pay plan. What they care about is whether you're human, whether you're someone they can connect with, whether you're someone they can share insights with. People care about you being willing to show some of your dysfunction, to be vulnerable enough to share with them, "If you're like me – if you're as messed up as I am – there was a chance for me, and there is a chance for you, too." This is what inspires people to sign up with you.

Release the Pressure of Perfection

At some point, you have to release your own pressure of perfection and give yourself permission to actually play this game. You have to find a way to have some fun with it in order to allow yourself to play the game long enough to get good at it. This kind of knowledge and skill is only gained through repetition and experience. This is the knowledge that you require to tap into your personal power. This is the knowledge that will allow you to market your own uniqueness and your own value, the value that only you bring to this game of free enterprise.

This is why the stakes are so high. Free enterprise is not just about wealth and assets; it's about you really reconnecting with you. It's about you finding out who you are. This is about you giving yourself permission to be the person you've always dreamed of being, to allow only the people who are attracted to you effortlessly to be in your circle of influence. It's not just about the money in your bank account. It's about your self-esteem, your self-worth, and your self-acceptance. It's about who you really are under that perfect veneer that you present to society. It's about truly letting go – letting go of your ego, dropping the drama, dropping the barriers, and letting people see and feel the real you – who you are now and who you've always dreamed of becoming.

The more you are willing to allow people to feel you, to connect with you – not just you connecting with them, but them really connecting with you – the more people are going to start to show up in your circle of affluence and influence. These are the people who want to buy from you. Regardless of what you have or have not produced so far, what you've romanced and haven't achieved yet, what you've dreamed and have achieved – it's just the tip of your iceberg. Celebrate the fact that you're in the process of growth, transformation, relearning your identity, and reconnecting with yourself. Be absolutely committed to the belief that there are no failures in this game. There are only experiences to learn and earn from!

INTEGRITY

Integrity is a character trait that will greatly enhance your odds for long-term success in business and in life. Integrity means being able to walk your talk. I am sure you have heard the saying "It does not matter if you can talk the talk, what matters is if you can walk the walk." Taking this adage one step further, I believe that it is important to keep our business transactions in alignment with our personal morals and ethical codes, as well as to create an awareness of what is actually happening in reality as opposed to our intentions. Walking your talk means that your actions in business align with your moral principles and that you scrutinize yourself and your business practices as scrupulously as you do the companies you do business with. It is very easy to criticize another business' policies and procedures, especially when they do not create the results you desire as a customer. As a sales professional, it is now your responsibility to look objectively in your mirror to ensure that you are aware of how your enterprise is actually operating.

When enter the sales arena, your personal integrity as well as the integrity of your business will greatly enhance your odds of being successful. One of the benefits of starting your own business is that you have the opportunity to create a company that operates by the principles you believe in. Your business can operate as efficiently and as ethically as you desire. You have the opportunity to create an enterprise that actually delivers the results you have been seeking as a customer from other businesses. Have you ever purchased a product from a company whose customer service was less than satisfactory? In the era of phone trees and automated systems, you have the opportunity to recreate the human experience within your business. Once you have set the ethical structure of your organization, its effectiveness, which applies to all human realms, can be learned. This comes from being conscious of how you use your time, leveraging your natural strengths, prioritizing, and learning to make better decisions.

Operating within your integrity is important because it requires far too much energy to maintain the façade that is created to legitimize your enterprise to the world when you are not in your integrity. I assist entrepreneurs and salespeople every day who expect their collaborators to take action that they are not willing to take and then wonder why no one is producing. I also assist great people who have found a way to dodge the system to create results. They end up making shaky and shady business decisions because they buy into the opportunity to receive short-term results without first considering the possible long-term ramifications. Then they spend enormous amounts of time creating the illusion of legitimacy and end up exhausted. The simplest way to succeed is to operate within your integrity. You may not always create the fastest results, but I guarantee the results you achieve will create a strong foundation to support your enterprise when it flourishes.

The number one reason businesses lose clients is the inability to follow through and deliver what they promise. One of the easiest ways to create a niche for yourself in free enterprise is simply saying what you will do and doing what you say. You want to create a niche you can produce and flourish in because this is what will separate you from your competition. Reliability is a very good niche to establish and maintain. It will also create a unique value for your enterprise because doing what you say is the epitome of great customer service. When you become known for outstanding customer service and absolute reliability, clients, revenue, and opportunity will flow to you abundantly and effortlessly. You will receive great referrals and get exposure to large networks of people because your commodity is so rare. Suddenly, the price of your product or service becomes irrelevant, because the value you are providing through your service is unequalled in your market.

You want to learn the art of under-promising and over-delivering. It is a very human quality to desire to "wow" your consumers and to promise them the moon and the stars to do so. The challenge with this impulse is that you put yourself in a position where it becomes impossible to deliver what you promised. Your clients will be more impressed when you exceed their expectations than they ever will be when you just meet them. It is time to become more practical in your desire to please your buyers or collaborators. You want to make sure that the promises you make to your buyers can be reasonably fulfilled, creating room to succeed and be the hero instead of promising results you cannot reasonably fulfill, letting your customer down and leaving you feeling like a zero.

Remember, what is pleasurable is what we do! Begin structuring your enterprise in ways that allow you to enjoy the entrepreneurial process. Create expectations for your collaborators and clients that are easily met so that when you go the extra mile it is easy for them to recognize that you have so they can express their appreciation. Here is a very simple example of what I mean: Jeff and I take great pride in providing exceptional customer service to our clients. One way we do this is by responding to all of our phone calls and emails, as well as shipping all orders, within 24 hours. I will often respond to an email within minutes of receiving it, and will often simply call the client if my response would be expressed better verbally than in a written reply. Not a day goes by where I do not hear someone say, "I can't believe you actually called me back!" My answer is always the same, "Why? Don't you feel you deserve a response?"

One-on-one personal attention and customer service is practically unheard of in today's business world, especially from the president or vice-president of a corporation. And yet, without our clients there would be no corporation. When you apply the Golden Rule to your profession, treating others as you wish to be treated, you create an entirely different experience for yourself and your consumers and collaborators.

Here are seven simple characteristics of integrity to consider when evaluating yourself and your sales career:

Release the Urge to Imitate

It can be very appealing to copy or imitate what you perceive to be a flourishing enterprise in your industry, just as often it is enticing to imitate the style, haircut or image of someone you admire. I call this "the grass is always greener" mentality, meaning "If only I were more _____, then _____ would be less effort." Let me be the first to tell you that when you judge a book by its cover you miss a lot of the internal content. An image is exactly that – a premeditated display of what someone or another company wants you to see – their glorious façade. There is nothing wrong with this either; it is also known as putting your best foot forward. We all do this and since we never get a second chance to make a first impression, we will continue this practice.

Resist the temptation to criticize and judge yourself based on your perception of another person or another enterprise. Success is not a competitive race, with one winner and many losers. Success is a process, and within the sales industry you have the opportunity to finally receive the recognition for your brilliance you have always sought, provided you remain genuine as you go through the process. Your uniqueness is the intrinsic spiritual value you bring to life, and this is what can allow your enterprise to produce massive results.

Celebrating your uniqueness allows you to be genuine in your collaborations and allows you to attract clients who recognize and value you for who you are. It is so much easier to relax and produce from your genuineness than it ever is to maintain a veneer disguising the real you. The same goes for your enterprise. You may not always top the charts in expansion, growth, or revenue, but your enterprise can always operate within your integrity so that you can feel good about the results you do achieve.

Set the Standard Instead of Rising to Meet It

Every industry has a standard of quality that is deemed acceptable in the marketplace. Take pride in your product and your service. Create a conscious choice to become a leader in your industry by setting the standard of excellence, rather than settling for consumer acceptance. This will require vision, creativity and belief that you are able to create in reality what you see in your vision, even though it has never been done before, period, or it hasn't been done in the way you are envisioning. Stimulating your creativity and vision requires you to disconnect from the noise of day-to-day living. This will require time away from your television, radio, and even time away from family and friends if their vision is not as encompassing as yours. Create an arena where you can excel in your industry, even if only in one aspect. If you are willing to provide yourself with this space and permission to flourish, your rewards will greatly outweigh your sacrifices.

Thomas Edison attempted more than 10,000 different applications of his vision before his creativity "tuned in" on the right combination to perfect the incandescent light. He experienced a similar experience when he created the phonograph.

On your journey, you will attract both supporters and naysayers. It is your choice whose input you resonate with. Setting the standard requires your courage to cling to the top of the ladder, which is never crowded, and then to deliver the message of what you see to those clinging to the rungs below you. Be prepared for some fall out and attrition. This is the part of the process of capitalizing on your brilliance. Be willing to let the opinions of others go so you can pursue your dreams. I guarantee that when you release your emotional connection to the masses, you will begin to attract the classes, and it is through the classes that you can set a new standard of excellence.

Truth – Why We Perceive It Hurts

Who created the idea of "brutal honesty"? Why do we as a society resist the idea of candidness and sincerity when we conversely complain of living in a world of corruption and deception? Why do we resist taking an objective look into our emotional mirrors when we already know what our reflections will reveal?

One of the greatest fallacies we create as humans is the idea that we have perfected any one aspect of our existence. I have learned in my own growth and development that is just when I am feeling smug and satisfied with my knowledge or insight about a certain situation that I receive an encounter or situation to completely negate my position and am very effectively removed from my soapbox.

The truth can absolutely set you free emotionally, and it is your emotions that act as your cause, driving the effect of either your action or inaction. It is time for you to be honest with yourself abut why you seek entrepreneurial success and what you will do if your dreams manifest, as well as what you will do if they do not. Regardless of our brilliance, there are no guarantees in this world. The only situations we can rely on are those we create through our emotional dialogue with ourselves, and the emotional expectations we create and expect to experience in return. Understanding your motivations and perceived pressures can also allow you to stop taking yourself so seriously. One of the most liberating experiences I have created is to laugh at myself when my emotional expectations are overwhelming my current experiences. This requires the courage to be honest with myself, not only recognizing my feelings, but also determining if they are in alignment with what is really happening around me. This is the truth of experience; when you can look at life from this perspective with a level of objectivity, your pressure to perform perfectly can be released and your permission to be yourself and to consciously create your experiences can be revealed.

Learning for Life

Have you ever noticed that just when you feel you have a particular situation all figured out, life throws you a curve ball as if to prove to you how little you actually understand? Regardless of your entrepreneurial experiences, sales skills or ability to communicate with people, you will find that free enterprise is a process of continuing education.

Life is in a constant state of transition and it is only your perception that makes you believe that a situation is static. The more you continue to grow and develop, the easier it typically is to stay in the flow of life's transitions. It is your willingness to receive the information from each experience and incorporate this information into your awareness that allows you to stay in the flow of your own evolution.

Your willingness to learn, grow, and change will enhance your experience, not only as an entrepreneur, but also as a human being. There will always be someone who has had more experience or created more results in your entrepreneurial arena. This is the exact person whose collaboration or mentorship would allow you to progress toward your goals more effortlessly. It is natural to resist learning from someone we perceive as competition, but when you allow yourself to stop comparing yourself and your results to others, you will find that there is never any competition in collaboration. Your willingness to learn from someone else also opens the door for them to receive valuable information from you in return. Success is a collaborative process; you require the support, knowledge, and skills of other people to create a flourishing enterprise.

The moment you feel resistance to connecting with someone you can learn from, you want to check in with yourself and ask, "Is this resistance in alignment with my integrity?" Stop for a moment to consider if this person in your present reality reminds you of someone from your past, both physically and emotionally. When you have made this connection, forgive your past experience that would sabotage your present opportunity, and let it go. Consciously connect with the person or information you can receive to continue your entrepreneurial education. The game of free enterprise offers no finish line, and the school of knowledge offers no diploma or graduation date. In this game you are offered the opportunity for success through your experiences in the process and the insights you gain there. The more you are willing to learn, grow, and change, the easier it will be to travel this journey and to stay in your integrity.

Knowing When Not to Compromise

In a compromise, both parties mutually concede to create a resolution satisfactory to both. In a true compromise, each party concedes something the other side finds acceptable. A compromise does not always create a win-win situation, but it does create space to move forward. Business requires compromise; the ability to negotiate a "yes" is a valuable skill to develop.

It is also important that you understand where your boundaries lie in business. You will learn this through repetition and experience as you develop your enterprise, but it is also necessary to determine where your lines are drawn in accordance to your ethics. These are the lines that, regardless of the situation, you will not cross; you will not compromise your moral and ethical code.

Developing this code in your enterprise will assist you to stay in your integrity as an entrepreneur just as it does in your personal life. When you are conscious of these boundaries, you will learn to gracefully withdraw from potentially controversial situations. The more controversy you are able to neutralize or avoid, the less you will attract drama and chaos to your business.

Defining Your Values

Defining your values is one of the key components to integrity. Values develop out of our emotional connection to our experiences with people who are important to us, particularly our parents. Understanding your values and how you created them is imperative

Am I open to receiving feedback to assist my development?

How have I improved my ability to create service and value?

How can I change the way I use my time to become more effective?

Does my conduct toward my associates and clients induce the respect I seek?

Are my business decisions in alignment with my conscience?

If I were to collaborate with or purchase from me, would I find the experience satisfying?

Am I in the right vocation? If not, why? What would I rather pursue?

What have you learned through this analysis? The purpose of this exercise is to create a very clear picture of where you have progressed and where you require development. With this clarity you can determine if your perception of your personal development and entrepreneurial effectiveness aligns with your results. You may find that your results exceed your perception or perhaps you have perceived a higher level of effectiveness than your results indicate. Perhaps your self-analysis has returned exactly the information you expected to receive. Regardless of your discovery, this exercise is a very effective method of checking in with your integrity periodically as you continue your journey in free enterprise.

HOW DID I GET HERE?

There are significant differences between women and men in business, and this often leads to communication errors. The more we understand about each other and how we interact with each other, the easier it becomes to do business. Just think about all the times that as a woman you may have miscommunicated with a man or vice versa. How empowering it is to understand the thoughts, attitudes, and emotions of the opposite sex, as well as recognizing the disaster areas to avoid.

A Difference in Perception

One of the first starting points to begin to understand the differences between men and women is to understand our different perceptions. Men and women perceive the same world through very different eyes. A man sees objects and their relationship to each other spatially, as though he were putting together a jigsaw puzzle. A woman takes in bigger, wider pictures and sees the fine detail, but an individual piece of the puzzle and its relationship to the next piece are more relevant to her than their spatial positioning. Male awareness is concerned with getting results, achieving goals, status, and power, beating the competition, and getting efficiently to the bottom line. Female awareness is focused on communication and cooperation, harmony, love, sharing, and relationships. This contrast is so great, it's amazing men and women can even consider living together in the first place.

Boys and Girls Respond Differently from Infancy

Boys tend to like things, and girls tend to like people. Girls' brains are wired to respond to people and faces, while boys' brains respond to objects and their shapes. Studies of babies that are a few hours to a few months old all show this one clear point: Boys like things; girls like people.

Scientific, measurable differences between the sexes show how boys and girls perceive the same world through the bias of their differently wired brains. Baby girls are attracted to faces and maintain eye contact two to three times longer than boys, while baby boys are more interested in watching the movement of a mobile with irregular shapes and patterns than focusing on a face at twelve weeks old. Girls can distinguish pictures of family from strangers, while boys cannot, but boys are better at locating a lost toy. These differences are obvious long before social conditioning has had a chance to take effect.

Preschool children were tested with binocular viewers that showed objects to one eye and people's faces to the other eye. A test of the children's recall showed that girls remembered people and their emotions. The boys recalled more about things and their shades. At school, girls sit in circles talking, each mirroring the group's body language. You usually cannot identify a leader. Girls are taught to seek relationships and cooperation.

Boys are taught to seek power and status. If a girl builds something, it is usually a long low-profile building with the emphasis on the imaginary people who are in the building. But when boys build something, they compete to build the highest and the biggest structure. Boys run, jump, wrestle, and pretend they're airplanes or tanks, while girls talk about which boys they like or how stupid some of the boys look. At preschool, a new girl is welcomed by other girls, and they all know each other's names. But a new boy is usually treated indifferently by other boys, and he is included in the group only if the hierarchy feels he can serve a useful purpose.

At the end of the day, most boys don't know the new boy's name or details, but they know how good or bad a player he was. Girls welcome and except others and are sympathetic to someone with a handicap or a disability, while boys are likely to ostracize and victimize the disadvantaged person. Despite the best intentions of parents to raise boys and girls in the same way, brain differences finally decide preferences and behavior. Give a four-year-old girl a teddy bear, and she'll make it her best friend. Give it to a boy, and he'll dismember it to see how it works, leaving it in pieces and then moving on to the next toy.

Boys are interested in things and how they work, while girls are interested in people and relationships. When a group of friends talk about a recent wedding, the women talk about the ceremony and the people who attended; the men talk about the bachelor party. Now keep in mind these are all general comparisons, and there's room for differences within each and every one of us because of our uniqueness and individuality. In fact, I have pictures of myself as a two-year-old dismembering and taking apart a plastic toy in such a way that there was no way to put the toy back together, because I wanted to see how it worked and how it was put back together.

Men Compete, Women Cooperate

One of the biggest challenges for us as entrepreneurs in businesses is that men compete and women cooperate. This too stems back to childhood roots.

Girls' groups are cooperative. Girls will ostracize a girl who asserts authority by saying, "She think she's somebody," or they'll call her "bossy." Boys' groups have a hierarchy with well-defined leaders who can be identified by their superior or assertive talk and body language, and each boy competes for status within the group. Power and status are all-important in a boys' group. This is usually achieved by a boy's skills or knowledge or by his ability to talk to others or fight off challengers. Girls are happy to build relationships, while boys question relationships. Instead, boys prefer to explore the spatial relationships of the world and generally do so alone.

So, what this means to us now that we're all grown up and in business together is that men compete and women collaborate. With men, there is a constant subconscious desire for competition to determine who is in charge and who's going to have command of the relationship. Women have been conditioned since girlhood to be collaborative. Being the leader, being the producer, being the person in charge is not nearly as important as maintaining the emotional congruency of all of the relationships so that no one's feelings get hurt and no one gets left out.

Where this really comes into play in business is when a type A personality man – a strong, competitive, dominant, producer, go-getter – confronts a woman and she backs down, because she's afraid that by confronting the confrontation she will sabotage the communication and therefore sabotage the relationship. And then the man looks at the woman and thinks, "Well, she's a pushover.

She's not someone I can respect. I'm looking for someone strong and powerful, someone who I know can lead me, someone who can, when the line is drawn, when the gauntlet is thrown, not just show up, but push through the battle lines and do it better than I can." And this is what often creates disharmony and discrepancy within our relationships in business.

A lot of times when a man challenges a woman in business, it is simply to determine how the hierarchy of the relationship is going to work. It has nothing to do with you personally. At the same time, men must realize that many times in business women will put their true feelings and opinions on hold in an attempt to salvage the relationship. It's very important to understand just what modern men and women are seeking – not just in personal relationships but in business relationships as well.

What Do Men and Women Really Want?

A recent study conducted in five Western countries asked men and women to describe the kind of person they would ideally like to be. Men overwhelmingly chose adjectives such as bold, competitive, capable, dominant, assertive, admired, and practical. From the same list of adjectives, women chose loving, generous, sympathetic, attractive, friendly, and giving. Women rated being of service to others and meeting interesting people high on their scale of values, whereas men rated prestige, power, and owning things as important. Once again, men value the tangible things; women value relationships.

There is a difference in the actual physical brain structure of men and women, and a lot of this dictates our preferences. What's important for you to realize is that for women talking about emotions and feelings increases serotonin levels in our body. This relates to the mind-body connection. When a woman discuss challenges, talk about problems, or work through why something isn't working with another woman, it actually makes her feel better, because she is discussing her emotions and verbally expressing what's been going wrong within her own brain. The neurons that wire and fire together in all of those connections actually increase her serotonin levels. They are feel-good chemicals, and even if nothing gets resolved, solved, or accomplished in the conversation, she feels better leaving the conversation than she did walking into it.

Men, however, increase their serotonin levels by the physical act of doing – by creating a result, creating change, doing something about the situation, finding a solution, and then implementing it. Simply talking about a problem increases a man's dopamine hormone levels, which means that when he leaves a conversation after talking about emotions and feelings with no action and no results, he feels depressed, tired, and lethargic. An emotional man can lash out like a reptile, while an emotional woman prefers to talk about what is going on.

For women, emotions operate on a more widespread area in both hemispheres of her brain, and so they can operate at the same time as other brain functions. This is why a woman can become emotional while discussing an emotional issue, while a man is less likely to do the same, or he might simply refuse to talk about the issue. This way he can avoid becoming emotional or steering out of control, because for men emotion occurs only in the right hemisphere of the brain.

A woman's emotions can switch on simultaneously with almost every other brain function. She can cry while changing a flat tire, whereas a man sees tire-changing as a problem-solving task (left brain), and remains dry-eyed even when he discovers by the side of a deserted road at midnight in the pouring rain that the spare is flat and he took the jack out of the trunk last week. This is why women can become more emotional and still create results, whereas a man will put his emotions on the shelf and do what's necessary to challenge the task at hand in order to get things done.

Women value relationships, men value production. Our modern society is merely a blip on the screen of human evolution. Hundreds of thousands of years of living in traditional roles have left modern men and modern women with brain circuitry that causes most of our relationship challenges and misunderstandings. Men, based on history, have always defined themselves by their work, production, and accomplishment; women define their self-worth by the quality of their relationships.

The man has always been a provider and a solution-creator, because this was his priority for survival. A woman has been a nest-defender, her role being to ensure survival of the next generation. All of the studies conducted on male and female values in the 1990s have continued to show that 70 to 80 percent of all men still said that the most important part of their lives is their work, while 70 to 80 percent of all women said that their most important priority were their families. If a woman is unhappy in her relationship, she has challenges focusing and concentrating on her production, and if a man is unhappy in his production, he has challenges focusing on his relationships.

Under stress or pressure, a woman views spending time talking with her mate as a reward, but a man sees it as interference in his problem-solving process. She wants to talk about it and he wants to do anything else but. To a woman, such a man seems uncaring and disinterested, while a man sees a woman as annoying or pedantic. These perceptions are the reflections of the different organization of priorities in the male and female brain. This is why a woman always says that the relationship seems more important to her than it does to her mate.

Understanding these differences will take the pressure off not only you and your personal relationship partner, but you and your business partners too. When you understand the difference between how women and men perceive the world and how each operates, you will be able to communicate more effectively, not judge each other's behavior is so harshly, and not take every situation personally. This has a lot to do with your entrepreneurial power and your effectiveness in the business arena.

The Wet Cat Syndrome

As I was coaching one of my awesome clients recently, we were talking about the Wet Cat Syndrome. I'm sure you've all seen a wet cat, or at least a picture of a wet cat. Wet cats are not happy creatures. They spit, they claw, they bite, they fight, and they do everything in their power to get away from whatever got them wet. They absolutely are not pleased with their current existence. And between a cuddly kitten and the Wet Cat Syndrome is the space of operation. It's the space of personal power. It's the space of personal presence. It's the space of understanding myself and the world around me, what triggers my reactions and responses, what gets my clock ticking and also what creates it to stop, and what sets the alarm bells going off.

Entrepreneurial Power

Entrepreneurial power means operating within your own emotional autonomy and your own emotional independence. It's giving yourself the power within your story to understand the differences between women and men and the differences in personality types. Entrepreneurial power involves understanding that it is not possible to create entrepreneurial success in a person-to-person endeavor without having other people that you can connect and collaborate with. This takes the emotional pressure off of ourselves in order to establish boundaries where we can be assertive, yet not aggressive. It's learning to understand the predominant personality types of the person we are speaking to so that we don't take their message personally, whether it's coming from a woman or a man.

To really become effective and assertive is to be able to let go of much of the emotional pressure on the outcome of every single situation. The biggest challenge so many of my clients face during the first three to five years of their businesses is creating results, because every result is taken so personally. I have clients that have been in the industry for years and have only managed to talk to 500 to 1,500 people. Becoming successful requires a lot more connection with other people than this to even begin to get good at this game.

It requires repetition and experience, and it requires that you set yourself up so you can receive that repetition and experience in a situation that doesn't create so much emotional pressure for you. This is why you always want to have more leads than you have time. You want to have so many people to connect with on a twenty-four-hour basis that you can allow yourself to gain new emotional perspective on your situation and not be so attached to the outcome of every single situation.

It really comes down to learning how to market yourself, your message, your value, and your uniqueness. How you market yourself will be different than how someone else does it. Each of us has our own story. We have our own personality. We have our own passion that inspired us to get started. We have our own unique message that we'd like to bring to the marketplace.

Partnering to Create Change

I've had the privilege recently to connect with many powerful women committed to creating a forum for women. We are collaborating to really increase the consciousness of women in the industry and to create more women millionaires than ever before. This is a cause that I am absolutely devoted to; I'm committed to contributing my time, my energy, and my information to assisting other women to create this forum, because I know unequivocally that the world would be a different place if we had more millionaires, especially more women millionaires.

I already know I'm not going to be able to do that myself, so I am always open to receiving other powerful opportunities with other powerful people to spread that message, to begin incorporating this idea of women and men partnering to create change. It's not about competition; it's about collaboration. Collaboration requires understanding the difference between how men and women operate so that competition doesn't stand in the way of collaboration.

Much of the above information references a great book, *Why Men Don't Listen and Women Can't Read Maps* by an awesome Australian couple named Barbara and Alan Pease. It's all about the brain chemistry differences and perception differences between men and women, and how common misunderstandings often create the situations that cause relationships between men and women to fail. It's very easy to interpret a man or a woman differently when you don't understand where they're coming from, and the flip side of this is that it's also very easy to understand our differences when we understand where other people are coming from.

Understanding the Four Personality Types

This is where the four personality types really come into play, because when you understand them, you can start to recognize which one of the personalities is dominant in the person you are interacting with. When you understand your dominant personality characteristics as well, it becomes easier to communicate and create relationships with other people. Jeff and I have broken down the four personality types into animals from the jungle in our eight-CD set, *Personalities for Success: The Animal Factors*. The four animals are the lion, the owl, the monkey, and the koala.

Our lion, the king of the jungle, is the classic type A personality. This personality type wants to be right, wants to cut right to the chase, get to the point, and go produce. Our owl is the analytical thinker of society that focuses on facts, figures, logic, and order.

Our monkey loves to socialize and have fun. The monkey is often vivacious and exuberant and not only brings life to any party, he or she often *is* the party. Finally we have our koala, the amiable relater and nurturer of society. These are the people who are interested in how they can assist others, those who will often make an emotional decision based on their feelings about you. The point here is that it's very important that you are aware and understand what to say to and what to listen for with the different personality temperaments.

Creating Emotional Space to Operate Freely

When you understand this, you can create the space in the middle between the cuddly kitten and the Wet Cat Syndrome. You can create the space for you to operate freely within your own emotional dialogue, within your own emotional state of affairs, where you know what boundaries are okay, what's flexible, and also what represents a deal-breaker – because we all have deal-breakers in business relationships as well as personal relationships. What I see happening far too often is that far too many of us acquiesce to too many deal-breakers, and then all of a sudden, one minor miscommunication happens and all of a sudden that minor miscommunication fires all of our emotions connected to the deal-breakers we've let slide. And then we end up reacting – typically overreacting – to what is really an extremely minor situation.

You see, that's when the wet cat comes out, spitting and clawing its way to justice, to proving its validation, to proving its being right. A lot of this stems back to emotional issues from our past that we carry with us into our present relationships, into our current business affairs. But here is what you want to ask yourself: not if can you afford to invest in letting these issues go, but if you can afford not to.

The Art of Having More Leads Than Time

I was coaching a client today, and we were talking about leads and what it would require in order to create more experiences with more people. And my client's response was, "I can't possibly afford to invest in more leads." And I said, "Really? Do you own a phone book?" And my client said, "Absolutely." And I said, "Great! Flip open your phone book to the white pages and start calling." Those would be free leads, and calling them would be called repetition and experience. That would be practicing the art of having more leads than anyone possibly has time to call!

Now, if you decide to open up your white pages and call people blindly out of the white pages, first of all, you deserve my complete respect and congratulations. But what you have to keep in mind is that these are unsuspecting individuals who have no idea that you're going to be calling them, so they deserve your accreditation. They deserve your understanding. They have no idea who you are. They have no idea why you're going to be calling.

Your return on your investment ratio of your time calling the white pages versus leads that you purchase, or especially leads you create, is not going to be stellar. But what it will allow you to do is practice the art of a millionaire habit. Millionaires prospect every day, whether they're prospecting for new clients or customers to buy their products –whether they're doing it themselves or they've hired a team of people to prospect for them.

This is what commercials are – a way to prospect the American populace to get them to buy Pepsi rather than Coke, Budweiser rather than Coors, Anheuser-Busch rather than Heineken. It is a great way for them to mass market to the populace. Most of us do not have the advertising budget of Coca-Cola or Pepsi Cola; that's why we market one-on-one, person-to-person. To really get good at direct marketing requires doing lots of it.

Let Your Heart Outshine Your Talent

This requires learning how to operate within your creativity and your outrageousness. It really requires learning how to let your heart outshine your talent. It requires letting go of being so perfect, of having such a perfect pitch that everyone you talk to can't help but sign up with you, and realizing that no matter how perfect or how effective you get, it is not going to be possible to enroll 100 percent of the people 100 percent of the time. There are always going to be people who prejudge the opportunity you're marketing when they don't have enough information to judge it in the first place.

You'll always run into people who prejudge the opportunity based on something about you or your personality type that triggers an emotion with them connected to someone else from their past that you happen to represent. So their emotions connected to an event and to someone else in their past experience gets projected onto you because you happen to have some of the same personality traits – it could be the same tone of voice; it could be the same area code. It could be something that reminds them of an experience from their past of someone they didn't get along with, someone they disliked, or someone they perceived slighted them. It could be any myriad of interpretations that they flashed to subconsciously, an emotional instance that takes them out of a practical awareness of really legitimately looking at what it is that you personally happen to be representing. This is why it is so imperative that as a marketer, you begin learning to take yourself out of this emotional equation.

The whole idea of personal one-on-one communication and marketing gets really complex really quickly, and it really breaks down very easily. The more you can understand yourself – why you do what you do, and why you feel the way you feel – the easier it is going to be for you to begin to create an awareness and understanding of the responses and the reactions of the people around you. Far too many of us take life way too personally. Free enterprise is an egocentric, soulless system, but your ego can become very narcissistic, thinking that everything that happens must have something to do with you.

The Law of Attraction

The law of attraction means that there may be times when someone else attracts you into their life to edify something they believe to be true about themselves that you resonate, so you show up in their life to prove them right.

It's not necessarily that you attracted them in order to prove you wrong. All of these laws require the space for you to remain emotionally independent and emotionally autonomous in your power in order to give other people the opportunity to become responsible for themselves, their feelings, and the situations that they create despite your best intentions to create a harmonic resonance between yourself and everyone that you interact with on a daily basis.

All of us have enough conflicts, challenges, and struggles in our lives without intentionally creating miscommunication with other people. You have to start giving other people the credit for doing the best that they're able to in the moment. You must be able to hire and fire yourself within the same day. You are always reinventing yourself as an entrepreneur. Give yourself the time and space you require to obtain the results that matter most to you.

Develop the Habits of a Leader

When I was involved in networking and direct sales, I actually did open up the white pages and prospect out of the white pages for thirty days. Was my closing rate outstanding? No, but I didn't expect it to be. The point was that I knew that my current habits were not going to serve me to create the kind of income results that I was seeking. At this time in my career, I was already doing four figures a month on a consistent monthly basis through my own product and retail sales, but I could see that I was creating a glorified job within my own business in this industry. What I wanted was a team of people marketing my business as much as I had been so that I could enjoy the residual income of their efforts as well as my own. That was the whole premise of the business that I was in. But I knew that I didn't have the habits, I didn't have the emotions, and I didn't have the habits of a leader in order to attract followers.

One of the habits of a leader that I have heard over and over again is diligent daily habits – diligent daily prospecting.

So I committed for thirty days to cold-call twenty names out of the white pages for seven days a week. That was 140 names a week for four continuous weeks, a total of 560 people. Out of those, I had a few express some interest. I never actually had any signups, but I did have some people show up on my website, and I did have some people show up on my conference call. Now, to be twenty-three years old at the time, and within my first six months in the industry already be creating four figures a month as a retail salesperson, I was ecstatic that I had this kind of result from my first cold-calling endeavor, using very simple scripts.

Success Is a Decision

Success is a decision; it doesn't just happen. Success is a process. But success is also a science, and the success is in the eye of the beholder. When you consider success at this point in your own entrepreneurial venture, it may differ from some of the leaders in your team. It may differ from some of your prospects that are looking at the business.

If you are seeking to achieve $1,000.00 a month, this averages out to about $33 in revenue a day. If your goals are higher – for instance, if you're seeking a $5,000 in revenue a month, then that's going to require that you generate about $167 worth of revenue on a daily basis, seven days a week.

If you are seeking $10,000 a month, this will require you to generate about $333 a day in revenue. This is how millionaires break down success and do diligent daily habits. They recognize what actions they require on a daily basis based on their skill sets, their communication abilities, and their emotional autonomy to average these amounts every single day.

If you're seeking $10,000 a month in your own enterprise on a monthly basis, the way is to first get to $1,000 a month. If you can get to $1,000 a month, getting to $3,000 a month is a lot easier from that perspective than it is if you are starting at zero. And when you're receiving $3,000 a month, it's a lot easier to up the ante to $10,000 a month than it is to focus on $10,000 a month with no results.

Getting Goals

Setting goals is important, but more important than setting goals is *getting* goals. It means creating achievable benchmarks on the journey of your life so that you become conditioned to practicing the art of success. This is one of the situations I assist my coaching clients to do, because goal creation and dreamboards have become so predominant within the personal development industry. Here's a news flash: I'm a rebel by nature. I don't write down my goals. I don't create dreamboards, but I do romance and begin to envision what it is I'm seeking to create.

Part of what I am seeking to create within the next ten years is a ten- to twenty-acre ranch on the outskirts of Stockton. This ranch is going to have a ten-stall barn. It's going to have an indoor covered arena. It is also going to have an outdoor sand arena. It's going to have a half-acre lake on it for my horses to experience water therapy via swimming, and it's going to have a first-class office compound, a first-class Spanish style stucco home with barns to match, and a twenty-five-car garage for Jeff and his car collection.

This is all going to come together because we are beginning to envision this property and exactly how it is going to look when it is finished. But I don't spend time creating a dreamboard about it. When I travel, I flip through magazines. When I see pictures that interest me I say, "Wow! That should be incorporated into my vision." I'll pull them out of the magazine, not for my benefit, but for the benefit of communicating my vision to the contractors that I'll be hiring when I'm ready to break ground on this project.

Ultimately, what I will be creating is a five- to ten-person workshop that happens on a weekend basis where you get to come and stay with me on my ranch, experience equine therapy, experience the self-esteem that begins to happen, and have the emotionally transformational experience of swimming with horses, of feeding a yearling colt out in the fields, watching its eyes go from wariness to trust as it determines you really are safe to be around.

This will be a place for you to experience how it feels to gallop bareback on a horse through a field of knee-high grass. Just imagine that picture as it starts to form in your own imagination. I know that not everyone that comes to spend the weekend with me is going to gallop bareback on a seventeen-hand horse going through a field of knee-high grass. But, my goodness, can you imagine the emotional transformation you'll have when a 1,200 to 1,500 pound animal actually succumbs to your will just because it's seeking to please you?

Steamer's Story

One of the things that I've gotten to experience over the last two years that has really increased my self-esteem and enhanced my power is seeing my horse, Steamer, go from a five-year-old who was underweight and undernourished and who wouldn't even walk even though there was nothing physically wrong with him. Three days after I found him and brought him home, he just gave up. He had no heart. He had quit on life, and he had quit on people.

He had no belief in the good that life had to offer. He had no belief in the value that he had to contribute to life. Yet this weekend, he is down in beautiful Carmel, California, competing in an AA-rated horse show. This is the top-rated horse show a state can host before going to national competition, and he's competing against some of the top horses from Canada, Oregon, and California. And he is loving every moment! He's jumping obstacles that are almost four feet high, and he is completely sound. And I'll tell you what, he has definitely found his heart, but this did require some courage. This required some faith. More than that, this required daily diligence and a lot of love.

In the same way, how willing are you to drop the drama of looking at your faults in order to really love yourself enough to enhance your odds at making it in this business? You've heard the old adage, "People don't care how much you know. They care how much you care." But before you can possibly care about anyone else, you are required to care about yourself. You have to release your myopic vision of seeing everything that's wrong with you so you can really recognize the good within you and begin to flourish.

What is it that you do right? What have gained from the experience you have had thus far in life? What are you able to bring to the world? What is the value of your message? How are you seeking to impact society by first impacting yourself? What guilt will you release to actually market yourself effectively to the world? What preconceptions of yourself could you begin to let go of right now to allow you to begin to create different results than you have thus far in your entrepreneurial journey?

Go Ahead – Reinvent Yourself!

Sales is about reinventing yourself each and every day. It's about practicing the art of outrageousness. It's about learning the mysterious, magical power of *you being you,* that intrinsic value that only you can bring to life and to this game of free enterprise. When you can capitalize on this feeling, the game becomes so much more than just about the money. The money happens, and it's great because it provides you with options, but it's also about the options you get to see people in your organization taking advantage of.

What about the options you could provide by donating great quantities of money to the philanthropic charity of your choice? What about starting your own charity? What about being able to start your own scholarship fund at one of the few colleges in our nation that actually offers a degree in entrepreneurship? What about becoming one of a million millionaires and having the kind of power to bond, mastermind, and collaborate with like-minded self-made millionaires to actually create changes within our society and our government?

We have a very disillusioned populace where many people are giving up on their dreams on a daily basis. But my friends, this is your chance to capitalize on your dreams, to capitalize on yourself. Don't miss the opportunity!

PRODUCTION

As you have experienced, or have begun to realize, salespeople get paid for results, not time. This is one of the most valuable situations you can come to terms with, and it is also one of the major keys to entrepreneurship that keeps most people stuck in their businesses. As employees, we are quickly conditioned to trade our time for dollars, settling for a wage that is based on what our employer has decided the task we perform on a daily basis is worth. As entrepreneurs, we have the opportunity to receive as much as the free market will bear in return for our energy, but our energy must be transmuted into a tangible product or service that creates enough perceived value that other people will buy it.

The Entrepreneurial Equation

The simple entrepreneurial equation is: $D + A - (EE) = R$

Decision + Action − (Emotional Expectation) = Results

In this equation, Decision is your reason for bringing you proposed product to the marketplace, otherwise known as your "Why." Action is what you are required to do in order to receive a return on your idea (i.e., how you will market your product). Emotional Expectation is the time frame you create for the results you expect based on your entrepreneurial experience. Results are created when the components on the left side of the equation fall into alignment. Results can also be called Production.

This is a very simple recipe for success, yet most people are challenged when it comes to taking action to produce results. In my opinion, one of the reasons struggle is so predominant in the sales arena is because we enter this game as adults, bringing with us a lifetime of previous experiences, most of which will not serve us when it comes to creating results in our own enterprises. Unless you had the benefit of growing up in an entrepreneurial family, you were not only conditioned to perform for approval, meaning a grade (in school), but you also watched your parents operate within their jobs, and all of this combined experience will not assist you to succeed in your own enterprise.

I have seen many successful, brilliant businesspeople fail as salespeople, and conversely I have seen the least likely candidate for entrepreneurial success flourish in the right opportunity. This just goes to show that in a free marketplace the only rules that apply are those you create for yourself. It is very simple to see that without production, results, meaning revenue, can be very elusive, meaning not present. Yet production is the exact situation most people both approach and avoid because of their perceptions of what it means and what it will require to achieve results.

Lower Your Emotional Expectations

One of the predominant reasons I see people struggle is that their emotional expectation of the results they expect themselves to produce is much too high. They decide to give free enterprise a shot, give it a try, see what happens, and hope for the best without a realistic expectation of the skills they require to create the results they seek in their enterprises. It makes logical sense that with a great product and sound business plan, an enterprise can be up and profitable in ninety days to six months. This is, of course, provided that every single element of your business and marketing plan operates in reality exactly as it prints on paper. Most people never take into account their entrepreneurial experience or lack thereof, or the human predominance toward procrastination, or the overhead required to continue operation while striving to achieve profit. Most business plans fail to consider the most important part of the equation when determining a business' success or failure in free enterprise, and that commodity is you!

Imagine how much differently you would have created your original expectations of yourself and your performance when considering the opportunity to create results as an entrepreneur if you had only known then what you know now. The great news is that as president, founder and CEO of your own enterprise, you have the opportunity to hire and fire yourself each and every day. You can choose to release your emotional expectations of yourself and begin to enjoy your journey.

What commonly happens is that we create unrealistic expectations of the results we will produce in a given time frame. When the results do not manifest as we envision, or the profit does not automatically begin to flow into our enterprises, we become disappointed and discouraged. The definition of the word *discouraged* is "not of courage," and you need courage to stay in the game long enough to produce results. As my husband Jeff says in his book *More Heart Than Talent,* courage is a commodity there is always a market for, and it never goes out of style. Success as requires that you have the courage to constantly reinvent yourself and to stay in the process of transition. Often, it is not the first marketing strategy or product we create that ultimately leads us to our promised land of financial freedom. Success requires the courage to stay in the process of transformation and development in the face of challenges and perceived setbacks. You will probably experience many of these on your journey, as all successful people do. These are not failures, but rather opportunities to gain the knowledge and experience to produce the results that will allow you to change the quality of your life.

The Opportunity to Design Your Life

As a professional salesperson, you have the opportunity to design your life. You have the opportunity to choose the experiences you will create while you are living rather than simply settle for the circumstances life hands you. It is important that you realize that we are all in a constant state of transition. Each moment of every experience gives us the opportunity to grow or to stagnate. The apparent stability of your situation or the apparent inability to progress is nothing more than an illusion created by your perception of reality. It is easy to become discouraged when the results you desire to produce do not manifest exactly as you expected, especially since we live in a society conditioned to operate within the confines of a job. The idea of free enterprise and the pursuit of living your goals and dreams is outside of most people's comfort zone, and they are usually more willing to validate your failed attempts than they ever are to commend your courage for stepping outside of the box of your job to manifest your desires as your reality. Understand that we live in a world that is conditioned to spend a lot of time worrying about problems, such as the war in the Middle East, escalating gas prices, the homeless population, problems with disease, the instability of the job market, etc. When you turn your focus toward the problems of life, it does not matter if the problems directly influence you or your family, or if the situations can be solved by you; either way, they distract your energy from creating change in your present.

Become Solution-Oriented

Producing results in any enterprise requires you to become solution-oriented. This means spending more time living in the solution rather than focusing on your problems. Doing this requires a different level of objectivity to begin to redefine problems as challenges. There is no right or wrong solution to any challenge you will face as a salesperson. You have the ability to create a solution based on your experience this far, and then you have the opportunity to learn from the situation created as a result of your action in the moment. Receiving a bill you do not have the money to pay in the moment the bill arrives on your doorstep can be a problem. As a problem, it is easy to perceive yourself as a victim of circumstance, saying to yourself, "How can I pay this? I don't have the money!" Objectively, it is also possible to receive this bill and say to yourself, "I am fortunate as an entrepreneur that I have the opportunity to produce results and attract this money before this bill is due."

The power of production lies in your perception of what you are able to create. It requires a transformation of focus from what you do not currently have to what you have the ability to create. When you can produce results, then struggle — whether financial or emotional — becomes a situation from the past. The ability to produce results also provides the conscious realization that you are in fact capable of flourishing in any given situation. This will require you to take action as if you are already producing the results you seek. A common misconception of our society is that you will not feel successful until you have produced the results that represent success to you. In reality, it is the exact opposite. When you allow yourself to act as if you have already achieved your desired result and feel the fulfillment of success, and when you produce from this emotional perspective, producing results becomes much easier and a whole lot more fun. Once again, when you are able to have fun in your enterprise and in your production it will release your resistance to the actions that create results.

After all, wouldn't creating more results in your enterprise open a new door to the solutions that would resolve many of your current challenges? Results are what will create the finances to provide you with the leverage to have more options in life; this is why production is so powerful. If you are seeking more results, become more productive with your time. Focus on revenue-producing activity instead of what keeps you busy. There is a time for paperwork, personal development and research, and that time is after the close of business for the day or early in the morning prior to the beginning of your business day. Shuffling papers, organizing your office, reading books, listening to CDs or tapes, or researching your company, product or opportunity is not what is going to produce results for you. Connecting with people, marketing yourself, and closing sales are where you should be focusing the majority of your time, especially if you are financially challenged in your enterprise. These are the three main activities that will offer you a return on your energy in a relatively short time frame.

Compensation for Results

Average people procrastinate and spend a lot of time in nonrevenue-producing activity, while exceptional sales professionals jump into the fray and produce. Procrastination is often due to unwarranted perfection, meaning when all your ducks are in a row and your office is totally organized and you have memorized all of the information about your company and product, then you will be ready to produce results. There is validity to all of these situations, but if you allow them to keep you from producing results, you will find that your progress will feel very slow because it takes you a long time to take action. In this game, you receive compensation in direct proportion to your results, not your time. You will not get paid for the time you spend perfecting your expertise and circumstances so that you are in a perfect environment to produce. Most people who get stuck in this cycle of procrastination and unwarranted perfection are so exhausted by the time they are done getting ready to get ready that they have no energy left to produce. As you can see, this is a very self-defeating situation.

As salesperson, you have the opportunity to receive results in return for your energy, provided you invest your energy in revenue-producing activities. This is the return on your investment. The difference between this return on investment and an investment you would make with a financial institution or as a venture capitalist is that now you can directly influence the rate of the return on your energetic investment based on how you spend your time. I guarantee that if you allow yourself to spend more time connecting with people for the next six months, your results will begin to quantify. I see so many people hide in their offices behind their computers and telephones. Yes, we live in a world where communication is greatly enhanced electronically, but the driving commodity in free enterprise is always people: the people you connect with personally and the referrals they bring you. This is about developing a network to enhance your net worth.

Create Great Connections

Creating connections is the name of the game for any business, whether it is brand new or reputable and established. Great people skills will allow you to have an entirely different opportunity to create results than the average person has. People skills are developed through repetition and experience, but most importantly, by learning how to listen. I have found that listening is the key to unlocking the mystery of communicating with other people, because it takes the focus off of you. I have learned to ask more questions during my conversations, and to create situations where I say very little about myself, instead finding out a lot about the person I am talking to. Because we all love to talk about ourselves, the other person leaves feeling like he or she just had a great conversation.

It is very common to feel uncomfortable communicating with someone you do not know because it is natural to worry about how that person will judge or prejudge you. It is also important to realize that your vision of yourself is probably a bit myopic, meaning you have a tendency to see only what you have not done, the success you have not experienced, and the situations you perceive as failures. I guarantee you that no one else would ever pick up on your emotional history if you did not broadcast it during your conversations. Less than twenty percent of how we communicate with each other is expressed through the words we speak. More than eighty percent of our communication is nonverbal, communicated through our tone of voice, body language, and eye contact (or lack thereof).

Last weekend I had the opportunity to observe 600 people at a convention where Jeff spoke. I spent the day at our sales table outside the meeting room, mingling and connecting with the participants who attended this event. It was fascinating to see how receptive people were to conversing with me when I was not behind our sales table. The moment they approached the table, however, almost all of them checked out of the situation. I asked them if they were enjoying the day and they said, "No thanks, I'm just looking," as they looked at the floor, the table, above my head, or at some invisible focal point over my right or left shoulder. I responded, "Since that's not what I asked you, are you receiving value from this event?" They would freeze, make eye contact, and then answer my question. Their first response was a knee-jerk reaction to what they perceived would be a high-pressure sales effort from me. My objective at our sales table is obviously to produce revenue, yet how can this happen if my customers are disconnected from the experience before we have even conversed?

Their initial response was not a rejection of me or a judgment of my ability to communicate. Again, it was a knee-jerk reaction that most people have when approached by a salesperson they perceive is going to attempt to sell them something. Creating results in this situation required that I first be able to see if these customers would allow me to neutralize their preconditioned reactions in order to receive a response to the question I actually asked. Provoking them to stop and listen to the question I actually had asked, rather than allowing them to blow me off based on what they thought they heard me say was a return on my energy; a return on my investment. The revenue was not instantaneous at that point, but I was creating a level of rapport with each person where they knew they could relax and have a conversation with me even if I was behind our table. This experience soon drew others to the table to see what was happening. The energy around our table soon became warmer and more positive, which in turn attracted more people to us to see what was happening. It's a good thing I did not take some of the first reactions I received that day personally. Developing great people skills to produce results requires that you stop creating situations to be personally offended by the reactions of people around you. It requires enough objectivity to understand when someone else's reflexive reaction is not about you, but about them and their emotional history.

Faster Is Easier than Slow

The more you allow yourself to stay focused on production, the faster you will experience the success you seek. Often, this will require multitasking in addition to great people skills. It will require you to maximize the action you are capable of taking in a shorter time period. Once again, energy and results are rewarded in this game, not time. I have taught myself how to respond to email and engage in a conversation at the same time. I can listen to a client, respond to the conversation, and type all in the same breath. This has taken over four years of practice to develop this ability. It is invaluable to me, because often a client will request information from me via email and I have the ability to send them the information in the moment and be finished with the situation as we end our dialogue. I do not take notes about what my client wanted, what email address to send the information to, and I do not add the task to my to-do list. Instead, the task at hand is completed in the present moment, allowing me to move on to other revenue-producing activities as soon as we are finished communicating. This practical application of multitasking skills allows me to create more results in less time. This means more revenue faster.

This should be creating an *aha* moment for you. It is much easier to prosper quickly than slowly. The journey to prosperity demands that you spend a lot of time on the highway of profit before you ever reach your destination. This is one highway with no speed limit and unlimited passing lanes. You can also either drive it or fly it! Are you ready to achieve results in your enterprise? Are you ready to see what the free market will bear in return for your energy? If your answer is yes, then it is time to release your perfection and move into production. It is time to stop buying into your current circumstances and claim your power to create your experience!

SALES POSTURE

Posture is another key ingredient in creating success. By posture, I'm not talking about how erect your spine is or balancing a stack of books on your head as you walk around your home. The information I have to share with you about posture relates to your conscious mental projections and how you resonate in life. You see, your posture is really your presence. It's how you project your energy, and the people you do business with will connect to the energy you emit.

Your Posture Is Your Presence

If you are constantly rehashing your past experiences, challenges, failures, triumphs, victories, or defeats, how much of your energy can you tap into in the present moment? If you are so anxious about what the future might hold for you, how much energy do you have left to create connections in the present? The answer is that you won't have as much energy as you need to create the connections and collaborations that will produce results in your enterprise. Attracting quality people to your business as clients or collaborators will require you to focus much more of your energy in the present moment. When your energy is present, YOU are present. This means you resonate from an entirely different frequency than the masses of society in order to collaborate with the classes.

We live in a universe where energy is neither created nor destroyed; it is only transformed. Every thought, every emotion, every particle of matter, every atom of your body is made of energy. Imagine what you could create if you allowed yourself to tap into that energy! Energy vibrates on different frequencies. For instance, a sound wave carries a different energy than a light wave, and a positive emotion carries a different energy than a negative one. If you seek to attract positive, motivated people to your business, then you must learn to emit the energy that will resonate with those people. When this happens, the people you seek will be drawn to you like magnets. This is because energy attracts energy that is vibrating at the same rate.

Your Posture Is Your Energy

Your posture—how you project your energy—has a direct impact on the people and the world around you. Every experience you have each and every day is a product of your expectation. That's how powerful you are! Your mind has the ability to send your expectations out to the Universe, and the Universe complies by providing you with situations to affirm those projections. This can be a tough pill to swallow at first, because it means accepting complete responsibility for the life you are currently experiencing. Remember, responsibility means *the ability to respond*. If you desire to change the people and situations you attract, the key is changing your posture.

I see people operating from seven key types of posture each and every day. It is essential that you begin to understand where people are operating from so that you can connect and collaborate with them without being affected by their posture in that moment. This means knowing how to neutralize someone's anger so that you do not subconsciously assist them to create another situation to remain angry. It also means neutralizing your emotions at times in order to capitalize on the posture of someone who is peaceful and calm. Your posture can absolutely either enhance your connections with others or sabotage them.

Over-Posturing – Too Angry to Connect

Over-posturing occurs when someone is too angry and aggressive to connect with other people. This type of person is constantly arguing and validating their position before it has ever been challenged. Over-posturing creates a tremendous amount of emotional and energetic distance between yourself and others, subconsciously driving away the very people you are seeking to connect with. People who operate from this type of posture often harbor a belief that they are not loveable or not good enough. They may feel that they were never listened to as children, so as adults, they perceive that in order to have their ideas, thoughts, and emotions heard, they must express them aggressively or else be ignored. Others perceive this posture as loud, rude, annoying, and argumentative. It can also be very intimidating if you are on the receiving end of this type of energy.

If you find yourself operating this way from time to time, it is important to recognize that you are actually sabotaging the opportunity to connect and collaborate with someone who could enhance your current experience. If you find yourself on the receiving end of this energy, realize that you are receiving the emotions of a hurt and angry child channeled through an adult body and mind; it's really not a personal attack on you.

Neutralizing this type of posture can seem intimidating. Let's face it, none of us enjoys spending time being angry or feeling the force of someone else's anger even when we understand it and are not taking it personally. It is important to determine exactly where your boundaries are—when enough is enough and when such a person no longer qualifies for your time if he or she continues to operate this way. Sometimes neutralizing this type of posture can only happen after one or both parties take some time and space to calm down. If you are the receiver in this situation, remember that the person operating from this posture probably has no idea how angry or aggressive they sound to you. If you respond in anger by becoming offended or defensive, your energy becomes combative as well. Now, instead of being in a situation with an antagonist and a protagonist, you will find yourself in a situation with two antagonists butting heads with absolutely no hope of collaboration.

You can always use questions in order to create space to determine if there is any neutral ground to collaborate on. You can say, "I can appreciate your position. What are you angry about?" A statement followed by a question works because it not only validates the other person's emotions, it also lets them know you are interested in *why* they are so aggressive or angry. I have used this tool thousands of times, and provided I am asking the question from my peace, I am able to disarm an over-posturer in a matter of seconds. Remember, this is someone who does not feel heard, justified or validated. Validating that you are indeed receiving their message loud and clear is a first step toward creating neutral ground to continue a conversation; just be sure to use this tool *before* you allow yourself to become offended by this person's attitude. If you wait until you are already offended and feeling angry and violated, your reaction will fuel the fire rather than extinguish it. This is why knowing your own emotional boundary is so important.

If you know that you yourself operate from this posture in certain situations, begin asking yourself, *What am I angry about? Who never listened to me? Whose attention have I been subconsciously seeking in life that I never received as a child?* These unresolved emotions connected to past experiences will continue to influence your adult relationships and business interactions as long as they remain unresolved. What happens is that we attract people into our lives to reaffirm the beliefs we've created as a result of a past event or experience. When you feel the urge to validate, justify or defend yourself, take a deep breath and give yourself a moment to relax and feel safe. Realize that there is nothing personal in business, and the only person you are ever going to be required to be good enough for in business is *you*. There is really very little judgment from others in the sales arena. It's the critical judge within us who creates many of our conflicts and confrontations.

Why is it even important to understand and neutralize an over-posturer? It seems as if this is the type of person you would absolutely want to blow off and release from your life. The reason is that many obsessive, compulsive, productive type-A personalities with unresolved anger issues operate this way unconsciously every day. These are also the driven doers of society, the movers, the shakers, the rebels, and the renegades – the very people who will produce from pride when the chips are down and the deck seems stacked against them. These people can produce the most results for you in your business, so if you can learn to communicate with and neutralize this type of person's energy, you can also capitalize on their strengths and abilities. You'll create the connection in this instance, but once it's established it often lasts for a lifetime because of the respect you create by confronting and disarming this person from your peace.

Under-Posturing – Too Meek to Be Heard

Under-posturing is the exact opposite of over-posturing. This is typically the posture of the great caretakers in society. Their message is, *Can't we all just get along?* There is nothing wrong with being amiable, but success in the free market requires you to project your energy with enough power for your message to be heard and felt by the people you are seeking to connect with. When other people sense that your posture is meek or submissive, they lose respect for you and your message. They may like you, but they will also naturally challenge you. They may become your friend, yet not buy from you.

I've assisted many of my clients with this amiable personality type to release their anxiety about what might happen in a confrontation with someone who challenges them. A-type personalities will cut to the chase and ask you questions like "What's this all about?" in the first 30-60 seconds of a conversation, especially when they sense you are someone they can challenge. I have found that most people who dread confrontation in any form do so because they have had negative experiences in confrontational situations. However, it is possible to confront someone in business without creating conflict. This is a skill developed over time through repetition and experience. If you feel people are pushing you around in business and in life, then it's time to create strength in your projection and begin demanding that your message be heard and acknowledged!

If you are too meek, begin to strengthen your posture by determining exactly where the lines are that you will not allow anyone to cross. This applies to personal relationships as well as business transactions. It can be easy to suddenly find yourself in a compromising situation if you feel guilty saying no or anxious about voicing an opinion that may conflict with someone else's. By knowing exactly what you will or won't do and what you will or won't settle for, you begin to create a new awareness of where these boundaries lie. By upholding them for your own personal integrity, you will begin creating the needed strength in your personal foundation in order to begin adding some power to your posture.

A great exercise is to scream into a pillow. Many people are too meek in their message because they are actually very angry inside and are worried that if they ever released any of this anger, they would explode and would never be able to stop. I've written more about this in chapter seven, The Power of Forgiveness. Screaming into a pillow provides you with a very safe and effective way to release some of the emotions you fear letting go of. It's safe because no one around you will hear you or be affected by your emotions. It's liberating to simply say what you feel, and you will be relieved to finally let go.

When you let go of whatever has been keeping you meek and playing small, you will be amazed at how much more effective your time and actions will become in your business.

Powerful Posture

Free enterprise is a competitive marketplace. There will always be someone at the top (Mark Victor Hansen, for example), and there will always be a new star on the rise. If you are the rising star on your way to the top, you want to be sure you have every advantage, and developing some power in your posture will greatly assist your assent.

This does *not* mean becoming rude, aggressive, or abrasive in your interactions with other people. I have personally met Mark Victor Hansen on numerous occasions, and he is one of the kindest, most philanthropic men I have ever met, with an absolutely genuine love of people. Yet he exudes an energy that commands respect from those around him. When he speaks, others listen. This is the kind of energy you want to develop as you continue your journey.

Remember that my definition of power is *emotional autonomy*. If you give yourself permission to be yourself, regardless of the circumstances, you have the ability to transform the energy in a room, or in a phone conversation. The following is a great example of how staying in your power and in your energy can enhance your results.

One evening after a live conference call, a woman from New York emailed us a question about purchasing the special package Jeff had offered on the call. She sent me the email at 11:55 PM her time, and I returned her message with a phone call within ten minutes. When I called her, she asked me pseudo-aggressively if I was aware of the time in New York. I replied, "Absolutely, but I can tell from your stereo in the background that your party just got started." She stopped, laughed, and said, "That was good girlfriend; let me go get my credit card!" In that moment, a potentially antagonistic [or adversarial] situation was neutralized and became favorable for both of us.

It would have been easy for me to have become rattled and have ended the conversation with this woman when she challenged me. Instead, I stayed in my power and found a creative way to neutralize her objection to the time of night I called her by letting her know I knew there was no way she was on her way to bed with the dance music she had blaring in the background. Her response happened to be very positive, but if it had been less than desirable, this would have informed me about the potential this woman and I had for collaborating. I have also had people request that I return their call the following day, which I have gladly done.

Developing a powerful posture begins with feeling good about yourself and your message. Once again, this is called self-esteem. When you feel good about your posture and your product or service, you will begin taking situations like these much less personally and will move into a position where you constantly seek room for collaboration rather than disconnection.

I have been involved in sales and marketing since 1996, and believe me, my posture then was much different than it is now, and my results reflected it. I have experienced the transition from a panicked posture of "How soon can I hang up and get out of this uncomfortable situation?" to the powerful posture of being able to neutralize a conversation to determine where there is room for collaboration. This transition happened through growth, development, repetition, and experience.

You have the opportunity to be an actor or actress in every conversation you have on the phone. If you do not feel powerful yet, act as if you already are! No one else will ever know the difference unless you tell them you are uncomfortable. Give yourself the power to say what you feel instead of reaching for the perfect response. This will allow you to be much more genuine, and it is this integrity of character that people will buy.

Passionate Posture

What are you passionate about in life? What motivates you? What gets you excited and brings light to your eyes? This is not about getting hyped, jazzed, or pumped up, but people respond positively when they hear passion in your voice and feel passion in your energy. What is your purpose, also known as your why? Staying connected to your passion, the reason you became an salesperson in the first place, will greatly assist your posture in the face of adversity on your journey.

When you are able to tap into your passion and resonate from this posture when challenges arise, you give yourself the power to immediately impact the potential outcome of the situation. Remember, energy projected attracts like energy back to it. It can be far too easy in this game to feel overwhelmed by adversity and give in to negative or self-deprecating criticism. Reconnecting to your passion during these times allows you to look beyond your current crisis to your long-term gain or objective.

It's the challenges you triumph over and the lessons you learn through your decisions that build character on your journey to success. I have yet to meet a successful person who hasn't bounced through a few chuckholes on the road to financial freedom. Perception is reality; your passion will be felt by others and they will be influenced by it.

I have a conference call series I host twice a year called "The Psychology of Releasing Weight." I began this forum when I realized that my emotions were holding my physical weight in place, not my diet or exercise habits. At one point in my life, I was exercising at my health club three to four hours a day with no results! I was living the definition of insanity by repeating the same physical actions over and over while expecting a different result. It wasn't until I changed my emotional dialogue with myself that my body ever had enough space to release. I'm sharing this with you because I remained passionate about my exercise routine and experience even while I was frustrated and looking for answers. The other members of my club could feel my passion for creating health in my body, and would let me know how much they enjoyed my presence in our group exercise classes, or down in the weight room. They said it inspired them to stay focused and motivated and committed to their own routines.

My point here is that success is a continual process, and there is always room for more growth and for more results. Staying connected to your reason for being in the process will not only see you through any challenges you experience on your way, but will also inspire those around you to travel on the journey with you. What a great support system! This is not about being positive, it's about feeling passionate. Passion will fuel your engine when you feel the train beginning to stall. Passion will create the momentum to carry you through growth to stability. When you project your passion through your energy, people around you will want to stay connected with you and will want to be a part of the business and experience you are creating.

Collaborative Posture vs. Competitive Posture

Collaborative vs. competitive—This may sound like semantics at first, but I have found that there is never any competition in true collaboration. I have had many opportunities to create what I believed would be a collaboration and then found myself in a competitive situation. I have also had many opportunities to collaborate and build relationships with people who could easily be perceived as direct competition.

Collaboration happens when the end result leaves all contributors feeling fulfilled and satisfied. Each person doesn't necessarily receive the same result because of the collaboration, but everyone benefits and feels good about the outcome. True collaboration is what creates the difference between building a business that has "flash in the pan" results and one that prospers and grows for the long run.

By default, competition will always exist in the marketplace. As you continue your journey, collaboration will not only separate you, the cream, from the milk, but will also allow you to build relationships with other people as you grow together. At times this may mean extending yourself for someone else to use as leverage as they grow and build their business. When you are able to do this in absolute faith that the other person will do likewise when they are able, you put yourself in a collaborative situation.

Competition occurs when one participant begins to perceive the objective as scarce and in short supply and actively demands more of it than the other. This objective can be money, opportunity, great people, connections, relationships, etc. Regardless of the resource being pursued, competition is created when one person becomes threatened that there may not be enough for both participants and begins to undermine the collaboration to receive more of the spoils immediately. In competition there is always a winner and a loser, and often competition sabotages relationships, creating enough discord to inhibit future ventures.

When you project a collaborative posture, you look at the long-term vision. You move into the situation willing to sacrifice short-term results for long-term gain. You focus more on building rapport within the relationship than you do the immediate outcome of the venture because you are focused on attracting like-minded people whose energy and goals align with yours. When this happens, you receive the opportunity to collect on the synergy of your efforts not only in the present, but also as you both continue to grow and develop. This can happen with individuals in different industries as well as those in your industry. Once again, this is about energy and projecting what you seek to attract. The more collaborative your attitude and posture becomes, the more collaborative people and situations you will attract.

Peaceful Posture

Peace is the key to resonating powerfully, passionately, and collaboratively. When you create peace in your own emotional dialogue, the tranquility within you will begin to manifest around you. Peace and chaos cannot exist in the same instant, and peace will neutralize and dissipate chaos in an instant. When you project your energy from your peace, you will find you are able to neutralize anger effortlessly, and any confrontations will not create conflict. You will find a different level of harmony in your relationships and conversations. This is when you can seek eye contact from another person and they meet your gaze willingly, feeling something positive is waiting for them in their experience with you.

Peaceful posture allows you to flow with life instead of creating resistance. It is the key to combining the three most powerful postures to create one ultimate frequency of energy to attract abundance. This is where you can hear the meaning behind the words people use and to respond intuitively to the emotional message you feel, not just the words you hear. When you are in your peace, you are able to respond to the situations you experience instead of react, and typically overreact, to them.

Each and every one of us currently operates or has operated from all of these different postures. There is no perfect posture to resonate from 100 percent of the time. Life will test you, and you will attract both positive situations to reinforce your development as well as challenges to test you. Decide where you desire to improve how you resonate and focus on developing the emotional foundation and skills to allow you to spend more time in that energy. You may have to have some experiences to teach you the lesson required to complete your shift in consciousness.

For instance, I have learned in situations where I'm feeling attacked or invalidated to stop and say, "I deserve better." If I feel I am not receiving the respect I deserve, there are instances where I actually make this statement out loud. Other times, I'll just say it silently in my own mind with the intention of creating the resolution I DO DESERVE. I have found that this is a very profound and noninflammatory way to draw a boundary about what I will and will not allow myself to experience. It is also a very powerful sentence that commands instant respect that I state from my peace to create what I desire instead of settling for what just happens.

If you begin to resonate from a posture that empowers you sixty to seventy-five percent of the time, I guarantee your results will begin to shift in your favor. Remember, perfection is not possible... this is about consistently choosing your reality to create exceptional results.

THE POWER OF LANGUAGE

As a salesperson, it is very important that you begin to study language and understand its importance in creating results. Language tells you a lot about the person speaking when you begin to pay attention to the messages behind someone's words. Your language is a projection of your thoughts, feelings, and emotions. Your words then lead to actions, which in turn create results. If you are seeking big results, it is imperative that you begin speaking an empowering language of success to assist you in accomplishing your objectives.

What Language Do You Use?

Most people give little or no thought to the words they use in everyday life. In my opinion, it is not a coincidence that most people who do not pay attention to their words are also willing to settle for average results rather than pursue exceptional outcomes. When was the last time you gave any thought to the language you use? Language is a powerful tool you can use to serve you on your journey. If your language has developed from a position of lack and scarcity, then the words you use will attract more struggle to you to perpetuate the reality you believe you are living in. If your language has developed from a position of prosperity and abundance, the words you use will attract situations and opportunities to you to validate this belief as well.

As I have stated, in our universe, energy cannot be created or destroyed; it can only be transformed. The words you use are a transformation of the energy of the thoughts, feelings, and emotions that you are expressing. The energy you project will be the energy you attract, and your results will manifest accordingly. This is why it is so important that you become conscious of the words you use if success is what you seek. I have realized on my own journey that successful entrepreneurs and successful businesspeople use a different vocabulary than those who struggle or barely get by. I have had the opportunity to spend time with many self-made millionaires, and they all share a common respect for the spoken word. They all are extremely aware of the words they choose to speak.

Words Empower or Disempower You

Your words either empower you or disempower you. Empowering words express a decision and a commitment, while disempowering words reveal hesitation, lack of focus, and inaction. If you ask me what one word you could release from your vocabulary to change your results, my answer would be the word "need." One definition of the word need is "a lack of something requisite, desirable, or useful." When you say, "I need to make more money," all you are speaking is the reality that you do not have enough money and that you are experiencing a lack of financial support. The word need has a very low level of energy, because by definition, a need expresses lack, meaning the situation can never be fulfilled. This energy then attracts situations and experiences to you to perpetuate your need so you can receive what you expect by never having enough.

Perhaps you find a new business partner or collaborator to partner with whose influence is going to open an influential network for you to create results with. You see how this one connection will bring you thousands of dollars, and then within a day or two you experience an emergency or some other major catastrophe which will require all of your expected revenue to fix. This situation continues to justify and validate your need for more money. Even though you were anticipating a great windfall, your spoke your need into existence and thus attracted a situation to perpetuate your lack of money. It does not matter how much money you are able to achieve if you are never able to retain any of it! As long as you perceive you need more, whether it is more money, more love, more opportunity, more recognition, etc., you will also consistently attract situations to you to negate what you receive to edify your original words and emotional position of what you need.

If you will simply replace the word "need" with the word "deserve," and develop the habit of saying "I deserve," you will notice that your results change. The word deserve can be defined as "to be worthy of" and once again, has a Latin root meaning "to serve." Deserve means to feel worthy to receive whatever it is you desire to attract. The statement "I deserve to receive more money" will create an entirely different experience than saying "I need more money." "I deserve more money" sends a message that I am worthy of receiving money to serve me in my purpose, thus I have no resistance separating me from the money I seek.

Do you feel how different this message is? Rather than projecting that you have a need, meaning a lack that by definition will perpetuate without ever finding fulfillment, you project, "I am worthy to receive exactly what I require to serve my purpose, and no resistance will separate me from it." If your purpose is to purchase a new car, you will attract the money to do so without also attracting a situation to divert the money you were going to use to purchase your new car to address a different issue. Instead, you will now attract the money you feel you are worthy to receive as defined by the word deserve so that you can use the money for its intended purpose.

Words Create Expectancy

In her book, *The Game of Life and How to Play It*, Florence Scovel Shinn writes, "A person, knowing the power of the word, becomes very careful of his conversation. He has only to watch the reaction of his words to know that they do 'not return void.' Through his spoken word, man is continually making laws for himself." What she means is that your spoken word creates expectancy in your subconscious mind, thus attracting the situation or experience required to validate your expectancy.

If you are having challenges digesting this concept, consider the psychology of superstitions. Carrying a rabbit's foot or a horseshoe will not bring you lucky situations in and of themselves. It is your emotional connection to the belief that these are good luck charms that create your expectancy of good fortune. This is also why Mondays are often challenging, while Fridays are easy. It is your subconscious expectation that attracts people, situations, and experiences to validate your current beliefs.

Words of Resistance vs. Words of Ease

I will assist you with identifying and replacing some of the most commonly used words that create resistance with words that will allow you to transition to nonresistance. There is a common misconception in our society that is must be difficult, draining, and time-consuming to produce the results which will enhance our lives and experiences. In reality, we receive what we subconsciously expect and speak into existence. If you have ever heard yourself say, "The only way to do anything right is to do it yourself," then it is very probable that when you assign someone else to a task, you receive a result from that person which is substandard to your expectation of a job well done. The irony is that you set yourself up to receive this exact situation through your previous statement. This situation can be neutralized instantly by replacing the disempowering statement with an empowering one, such as "I effortlessly communicate exactly what I expect so that when I assign a task to someone else they complete it exactly as if I performed the task myself." Do you see how much easier your life can become just by changing a few simple words?

WORDS OF RESISTANCE	WORDS OF EASE
Try	Will
Need	Deserve
Work	Produce
Hard	Easy
Maybe	Yes or No
Think	Feel
Yeah, Uh-huh	Yes
Nah, Nope	No
Cost	Value
Busy	Productive
Struggle	Effortless
Help	Assist

All of the above words of ease are words for you to consider incorporating into your vocabulary. These are words of prosperity and abundance -- emotional as well as monetary.

Here are a few statements I use in my life which have positively impacted my results:

New Empowering Statement	Statement to Release
I deserve to receive exactly what I desire!	*I need* _____ .
I am a productive entrepreneur!	*I am so busy!*
What is the value?	*How much does this cost?*
I produce results effortlessly!	*I work really hard.*
I require/seek assistance.	*I need help.*
I will.	*I'll try.*
How do you feel about this information/situation?	*What do you think?*

Words of resistance usually carry little or no commitment. For instance, if I asked you to try to stand up, you would have challenges performing this task. This is because you will either sit or stand. To say you will try something means you will contemplate it, but eventually take no action. When you ask someone if they will review information about your product or service and they respond with "I'll try," this is a clue as to what they are already telling you they are not going to do.

Learn to Listen to the Words of Others

To succeed in sales, you will be required (not you will need) to learn how to provoke other people to take action. Once again, most people are not aware of the words they use or how these words impact their reality. As you become more conscious of your own language, you will also become more aware of the words other people use. You will begin to hear the underlying subconscious messages behind the statements they make. For instance, if someone says to you, "This sounds good but how much does it cost?" you will receive an insight into their dialogue with money that they had no idea they were broadcasting. I learned very quickly when I worked in industrial diesel engine and generator sales that the price had absolutely nothing to do with the purchase. Until your client or customer understands the value of what you are marketing and understands how it will enhance their life, the sticker price assigned to it is meaningless. Until the value is ascertained, there is no incentive to buy.

In the previous example, you also are receiving a contradictory statement. If your opportunity or product sounds so good, where is the resistance coming from? When you begin to understand why we choose the words we speak, you will begin to communicate on a different emotional level. You will understand that price is never the issue; it is always about perceived value. If you are receiving objections about the price of your product or service, then you might consider changing the way you are presenting the value of what you are marketing.

Speak Prosperity!

Prosperous people consistently seek ways to add value to their experience. They do not focus on what a product or service costs, rather they focus on the value that product or service will bring. This is a very important distinction to understand, because when someone asks you the cost of your product or service within the first thirty to sixty seconds of conversation, this should give you a clue about this person's dialogue with money and prosperity. It is always easier to complete business transactions with emotionally, spiritually, or financially prosperous people because they already have the means to complete the transaction. What happens so often is that we feel intimidated by what we perceive we lack in comparison to these people and so resist approaching them with our product or service.

Prosperous people seek ways to add value to their experience, regardless of who presents the opportunity to them. If you speak words of ease and prosperity, you will capture their attention very quickly and they will be much more likely to buy from you. Your language will create a connection to bridge the gap between you. If you speak words of prosperity, you will begin to make deposits in your emotional and spiritual bank account and these deposits will eventually manifest in your physical bank account. How quickly this happens is entirely up to you. The thoughts you think influence the words you speak, which determine the results you drink!

THE POWER OF QUESTIONS

In every conversation, you have two options when you open your mouth to speak. You have the option to either create a statement or ask a question. Learning to ask great questions is one of the most powerful skills you can develop in your entrepreneurial or sales career. Questions lead you to the answers you seek from the world around you and from other people. More importantly, questions allow you to examine your emotional self in order to gain a clearer understanding of why you do what you do. This questioning of self will lead you to the information you seek about the causes of your behavior so you can create the change in direction you require to create the results you seek. This information transcends the sales and marketing arena – it is applicable in all areas of life and relationships.

Each of us desires to believe that we have the ability and the power to change the direction of our lives. The challenge for most people is that between the glimmer of inspiration that provokes them to see what they are capable of and the actual manifestation of their dreams, reality sets in. In reality, setbacks, frustrations, anxieties, and perceived failures occur in the process of transition. These situations are normal and almost always occur for those who are in the process of change. The key to understanding this process and to neutralizing the negative feelings connected to them is learning to change your questioning habits in order to create a better understanding of what is actually happening. The questions you learn to ask yourself will allow you to begin to shift your focus from what is happening *to* you to realizing what is happening *for* you. Every situation, every confrontation, every conversation, and every experience is an opportunity to gain insight and wisdom into your thought processes and emotions. It is always the times of greatest challenge that create the strength and resilience required to flourish in times of ease and flow. These times of challenge and change also reveal to you why you behave and respond to people and life the way you do. As you develop a clearer understanding of your own psychology, you will gain tremendous insight as to why other people practice their own behaviors.

Learning to ask yourself great questions about what you are experiencing in life will lead you to better answers and better solutions. Better questioning skills will also lead you to improve your relationships at home, in business, and especially in your sales dialogue.

Sales and marketing is really about understanding what motivates people to buy. The questions you ask a prospective client will provide you with the information you require to understand the motivation this person feels to either buy from you or to wait and buy from someone else. They will provide you with the specific or necessary information you require to persuade or motivate someone to create a meaningful change in their life. Questions will allow you to command the attention of another person long enough to determine if there is a match between your product, service, or opportunity and what that person seeks. Questions are the key to communication; they open the door to communicating clearly, concisely, and comprehensively.

As the pace of our society continues to increase, the attention span of the average individual continues to shrink. Consider that we have more methods of communication now than ever before, but we seem to lack the time required to actually talk to each other. We have cell phones, cordless phones, email, instant messaging, fax machines, BlackBerries, pagers, voicemail, VoIP, and who-knows-what invention coming next. These innovations are designed to provide us with a greater opportunity to communicate interpersonally, but they also create more opportunities for misunderstanding and miscommunication.

In sales, people crave the human touch. No matter the vehicle people communicate through, the reason for communicating remains the same. In this journey of human experience, we require information. In order to gain this information, we must know what questions to ask and how to ask them. Acquiring information at the right time is as crucial in achieving sales objectives as building relationships with other individuals. Building better relationships begins with establishing rapport, which really means asking questions to receive better information to see where a connection can be created. This connection creates a bridge between you and another person, linking your commonalities and neutralizing the perception of distance between you. The faster you learn to create this connection, the easier interpersonal communication becomes.

The Seven Powers of Questions

1. Questions compel people to provide answers.

From the time we learn to speak, we are conditioned to answer questions. In fact, answering questions is a key component in practicing our speech in our early development. This conditioning begins as early as asking "What does the dog say?" and "What color is Daddy's car?" This early conditioning creates a reflexive response to answer questions – it is automatic.

We also learn that through asking our own questions we can demand answers from other people. As our quest for information and knowledge grows, so does our demand for answers to provide information about the world around us.

People answer questions for two reasons. The first is that answering a question is a reflexive response, and the second is due to what we are taught is cooperative and acceptable by society. There are rules that we all operate by, and one of them is that when someone asks us a question, they expect a response. Our conditioning teaches us to answer questions to the best of our ability in order to provide information that will show we are being cooperative.

This is why as salespeople we are often easily seduced into talking and launch into long and involved answers in a conversation. The key to capitalizing on this first power of questions is to learn to provide a small amount of information in your answer and then ask another question. As a sales professional, it is your responsibility to find out as much information as you can about your client or prospective buyer. This means you must learn to give less information and ask more questions. You must begin to recondition your automatic answering reflex and realize that in this game, providing the best information is not going to guarantee the greatest reward – asking the most effective questions will!

This provokes the question, "How do I ask effective questions?" Here are a few situations to keep in mind when asking questions to be specific in your purpose and gain the insight you require to increase your odds of creating a sale:

- Specifically, what am I seeking to gain with this question?
- Who am I asking?
- When is the right time to ask?
- What impact will this question have?

2. Questions provoke emotions.

In order to open people up to investigating their emotions, you want to always ask them how they feel about your product, service, or the information they have received about your opportunity. When people begin to talk about their feelings, they become connected to the right hemisphere of their brain. This is the part of their brain that is creative and open to new ideas and dreams. When people are connected to this part of their brain, they are much more open and receptive to a new experience. As souls having a human experience, we are all ultimately seeking an emotional connection with each other, and asking someone how they feel begins to open the door to this connection. Also, because most people are used to being asked what they *think*, many people will give you more of their attention when you ask them how they *feel*.

3. Questions provide access to information.

It is amazing that with as many ways to communicate as human beings have created, miscommunication is still prevalent in today's society! It would be an effortless world if the information we sought about each other were delivered with crystal clear clarity on a silver platter. These days, though, the information we seek is more likely to be buried in a stack of email, voicemail messages, faxes, and letters, not to mention the obscurity of the thoughts and emotions of others! All too often, we create decisions based on a hunch or a prayer that our insight is correct without having the crucial piece of information to validate our leap of faith.

Instead of falling prey to this common act of miscommunication, begin asking for more of the information you require. A simple "I am not sure I understand what you mean" can effortlessly provoke someone to give you more information. This is the information you require to determine a multitude of situations:

- Is this a valid lead?
- What is this person's motivation?
- What is this person seeking?
- Is this opportunity a match or a mismatch for this person?

And these are only a few of the very relevant situations where you require clarity to determine how long a conversation will continue!

4. Questions direct conversations.

Have you ever felt like you were out of control in a conversation that you initiated? We all have at one point in time or another. The key to conversing effectively in sales and marketing is learning to command a conversation through asking questions that will lead your prospect in the direction you want them to go. This means learning to ask questions that you already know the answers to. When you have an idea of how someone will answer your question before you ask, it allows you to relax – even when conversing with a stranger. For instance, if it is a clear, beautiful, sunny day and you ask someone, "Isn't this weather wonderful?" the odds are pretty good that person is going to agree with you, even if this is the first time you have ever conversed.

The same is true in prospecting! You want to begin to develop a repertoire of questions you ask each and every prospect or prospective client with a general expectation of the response you will receive. There are literally thousands of these questions that you can create over time to ask in your own sales process, but in the meantime keep reading to learn the top five questions you should ask in EVERY sales conversation to direct and command the flow of your dialogue.

5. Questions open people up in conversations.

There is a dramatic difference between asking questions that allow others to open up and reveal information about themselves and asking a series of closed-ended questions that feel like an interrogation. The key to asking questions that allow people to open up and converse freely with you is to ask open-ended questions. Close-ended questions can be answered with one or two word responses, such as a Yes or a No. Open-ended questions require more than a one or two word answer.

It is also very beneficial to incorporate a topic into your open-ended questions that allows the other person to reveal something about themselves without focusing on them specifically. Here is a great example of this kind of open-ended question: "What specific qualities do you seek in a company for you to consider getting started?" Another is "What value do you feel a product/service such as _____ (your product) would bring to your life?"

Questions such as these open people up primarily because most people love to talk, especially about themselves and what interests them. These questions get you past the facts of a conversation – past *who, what,* and *where* – and lead your conversation into *why* and *how.* When you begin to understand the reasons why people create the decisions they create and how they create them, you gain priceless insight into how and why they buy. As soon as you have excavated this treasure chest of insight from another person, the sales process becomes easy!

Here are several ways to begin allowing other people to open up in a conversation:

• Develop a good rapport with people by treating them as individuals, not as "clients" or "prospects." Create the time to spend just a few moments in polite conversation connecting on a deeper level than "How are you today?" You will be amazed at how thirty to sixty seconds of sincere interest improves the warmth of your conversations.

• Begin using general, open-ended questions. Allow the other person time to express their thoughts without interruption. As your conversation progresses, begin to ask more direct, probing questions. For example, you might begin a prospecting interview with a question such as "What has you in a position where you are looking for a way to achieve income from home?" Once your prospect knows there is room to communicate with you freely you can ask a more pointed question, such as "What specific talents and skills have you acquired in your life thus far that you feel would be an asset to you when you join our team?"

• Save the questions you feel are the most challenging for the end of your conversation. Remember that if someone is anxious about the consequences of opening up and telling the truth, they will be much more reluctant to open up and tell the entire story.

• Communicate your interest nonverbally. You can do this both in person as well as via telephone by leaning forward into your conversation. If you are sitting beside someone in conversation and you cross your legs, make sure that you cross your leg so that your body remains open to the person you are listening to. So, if your companion is sitting on your left, crossing your right knee over your left will leave your body language engaged and receptive in the conversation. When you are on the telephone, take the time to listen to the other person's entire answer before taking any notes.

Your impressions of what they say and the questions you ask based on those impressions are much more important than writing down exactly what you thought you heard.

6. Questions lead to quality listening.

As important as asking questions is, quality listening is the key to keeping a conversation flowing. When you begin developing your listening skills and paying attention to how other people listen – or rather, do not listen – you will see how rare and valuable listening skills truly are. Most people in today's world stop listening about halfway through the answer to a question – have you noticed this? Have you ever noticed yourself doing the same thing? Why are we, a relatively curious species, so eager to stop listening when the opportunity arises to find out about someone or something that provoked our curiosity enough to ask a question?

The answer is simple! We stop listening because we are already formulating what we will say when the other person has finished speaking. In doing this, we actually miss about half of the information we would have had the opportunity to receive had we stayed fully engaged in the conversation.

In sales, you cannot afford to miss a single piece of information your prospect or client is willing to reveal. One phrase, one word, even one breath or exhalation in a conversation can provide you with the insight you require to create collaboration or close the sale. When you miss these moments, you miss what great salespeople worldwide are listening for every moment of every day. What you miss is what other people mean, because you are only hearing about one-half to two-thirds of what they say. There is more context in people's meaning than there will ever be in their words, and you will miss their emotional dialogue if you are in your head, processing what to say next.

Yes, asking questions is imperative to creating sales success, but quality listening will allow you to capitalize on your great questions.

7. Questions allow people to persuade themselves.

Now is the time for you to realize that other people believe what *they* think, not what *you* say. Oh, what a blow to the ego, you cry! It is true, my friends. Regardless of our station in life or the credentials we carry, other people believe what happens inside their minds, not the words we speak to them. This means that it's the conclusions they draw during a conversation based on what we say that leads them to a decision – not our ability to wax poetic.

Has anyone ever tried valiantly to convince you of something you did not believe? Did your opinion in the situation ever change? If so, why? Was it your absolute belief in something they said, or was it something in the conversation that allowed you to consider what they were saying from a different perspective? In reflection, you will often find that it is a well-placed or well-timed question that can change the course of an entire conversation.

Realize that most of us are stubborn by nature, and we like to believe that we are right and that we know what is best for us. Most of us naturally resist when someone else tries to tell us what to do, even if their advice is in our best interest. Instead of wasting your time convincing someone else why they should change, next time ask a question instead.

Example: You really should buy a new car.

Question: How would your life change if you were driving a new car?

Example: You should sample our product to see if it assists you.

Question: If I sent you a sample of our product, would you be willing to use it to see if it adds value to your life? If you enjoy this experience, would you be open to reconnecting with me?

Asking questions like these is the key to mastering the power of persuasion. One way to do this for yourself is to begin paying attention to the statements you create that receive resistance from others. Create a list of statements over the course of a week. Then invest a few moments at the end of your week to change each statement into a question. Spend some time internalizing the different feelings each question elicits from you compared to the feelings connected to your statements. This will greatly assist you to incorporate more questions into your conversations where previously you would have simply created a statement.

The Five Questions EVERY Prospect Deserves to Answer

1. What has you in the position where you are seeking a way to create income from the comfort of your home?
2. How long have you been looking for an opportunity?
3. What is your present vocation? *or* What are you accustomed to doing to create a living?

4. Provided you find an opportunity that makes sense to you and you see an opportunity for yourself in it, are you in a position to get started now?
5. How much money have you set aside to invest in a business opportunity this year?

The Five Questions EVERY Client Deserves to Answer

1. What has you in the position where you are seeking a different product/service?
2. How long have you been looking for a change?
3. What product are you currently using? What do you love about it? What do you hate about it?
4. Specifically, what are you seeking in a replacement product?
5. If I could offer you a product that met your requirements, what value would it bring to you?

These are sample questions you can begin implementing to create different results in your enterprise. As you continue your journey, you will develop other questions of your own. The exact questions you ask are not nearly as important as the results you create because of the questions you ask.

You deserve not only the sales you will create through improving your questioning skills, but also the connections with other people and the experiences you will have as a result. Sales is not about what you do for a living; it's about what you do and experience while you are living.

SIMPLE SCRIPTS FOR SUCCESSFUL SALES

The purpose of this chapter is to introduce you to simple, powerful, and effective scripts to assist you in developing your ability to connect with your prospects, build rapport, increase your confidence, neutralize objections, and ultimately close sales. Entire books have been created on the concept of sales scripts, with good reason! There is a tremendous amount of power connected to having effective words at your fingertips (and eventually using them automatically) in the exact moment you require them. When used effectively, scripts can assist you to develop a command of your selling experiences and greatly improve your ratio of sales opportunities to successfully closed sales.

It is also important to keep in mind that a script is merely a map to follow in a conversation. If you are traveling from point A to point B in a city you are unfamiliar in, you will use a map to guide you in your direction. You will also notice as you begin studying your map that there are many different routes you may choose from, depending on the experience you are seeking during your journey. For instance, if you prefer to enjoy the peace and quiet of the rural countryside you probably would not choose to drive through the urban area in this city – instead you would enjoy less traveled country roads even if the urban route would get you there faster!

Just like geographical maps, many different people may interpret the route in a conversation from point A to point B differently. These scripts are designed to provide you with a guide, a simple map to begin with as you navigate your conversations in sales – what may be unfamiliar territory. Even the best sales professionals are always seeking ways to enhance and improve their communication skills as well as their ability to navigate to a sale with the least effort in the shortest amount of time.

Remember that, like an actual road map, these scripts are designed for you to refer to when you require guidance. If you simply stare at them and use them verbatim word for word, you may find yourself in a sales accident! Imagine what would happen if when driving your car you never looked up from the map to steer! This can also happen in a conversation, and it will happen if you are so focused on your script that you forget to listen to your prospect!

This is why these scripts are short, sweet, simple, and to the point. My goal for you is to feel motivated by this information to prospect and connect to achieve the prosperity you desire and deserve in your enterprise. Because they are simple, they are easy to memorize, and as you do so, they will feel so comfortable that in no time you will feel as if you have been speaking this way your entire life!

Message to Leave on Your Personal Voicemail Greeting *(Created by Jeffery and Erica Combs)*

Hello, you have reached the office of _____. Congratulations on your call today! Our organization specializes in assisting people from all walks of life to create income in their own businesses, on their terms and in their time frame.

If you have been searching for a legitimate, home-based business that could put you back in command of your finances, your freedom, your time, and your life, then you will definitely want to learn more about this business opportunity.

The members of our community are creating wealth from the comfort of their homes with a globally recognized company that can assist you to generate the income you deserve on your own terms.

Please leave your name and your phone number twice and be sure to include your area code and the best time to contact you. Your call will be returned personally within twenty-four hours by either myself or one of my qualified associates.

We look forward to connecting with you to determine if you have some of the necessary qualifications to be a member of our rapidly growing team.

What we will not do is try to sell or convince you to get started with our company. What we will do is share more with you about this income opportunity, providing you with the information you require to make an educated decision about changing the quality of your life.

Remember, please leave your name and phone number twice with your area code!

Thanks for calling and YOU create a very prosperous day.

Message to Leave on Prospect's Voicemail

Hello, this is a message for _____.
My name is _____, and I am calling from _____
(your city and state).
The purpose of my call is that you have responded to information about creating an additional stream of income from the comfort of your home.
If this is still correct, my direct number is _____ (your 800 voicemail box). I look forward to receiving your call and connecting with you.
Thank you for your time and YOU have a very prosperous day.

Message to Leave on Referral's Voicemail

Hello, this is a message for _____.
My name is _____, and I am calling from _____
(your city and state).
We don't know each other personally, but your name and number were referred to me by
_____ (person's name who gave you the referral) as someone who is an opportunity seeker like me and open to looking at a way to increase your income from the comfort of your home.
If this is still correct, my direct number is _____ (your 800 voicemail box). I look forward to receiving your call and connecting with you.
Thank you for your time and YOU create a very prosperous day.

Easy "YES" Script (GREAT for Three- Foot Rule Prospecting)

Hello, has anyone ever told you _____? (Heartfelt compliment here)
Ex: you have great energy; you are a great multitasker; your energy lights up the room, etc.

My name is _____, and I am always looking for quality people like you to join my team.

Does the opportunity to create an additional stream of income this next year appeal to you?

They say YES:

Great! Would it be possible for us to exchange contact information so we can connect when we have more time to talk?

Exchange cards or have them write their information on the back of one of your cards.

Thank you! I will definitely follow up with you in the next twenty-four to forty-eight hours. It was a pleasure meeting you!

Live Prospecting Callback Script

Hello, may I speak with _____?

Hello _____, this is _____ (your name) from _____ (city, state). How are you today?
I am glad I reached you. The purpose of my call is that you responded to my advertisement and listened to a message regarding achieving an additional stream of income from the comfort of your home. Is this still correct?
Alternately:
I am glad I reached you. The purpose of my call is that you responded to information about achieving an additional stream of income from the comfort of your home. Is this still correct?
Great! Once again my name is _____, and the company I represent is

_____ (your company). Have you ever heard of us?

If your prospect says Yes:

Really? How did you find out about us?

If your prospect says No:

In a nutshell, we are a group of like-minded entrepreneurs that have collaborated for several reasons: the strength of numbers, security, longevity, and prosperity for all of us.

We're looking for a few quality individuals to join our marketing team. All results are created via the telephone, and I am seeking people with two qualities: moderate people skills and lots of desire.

Is this you?

This is where you stop talking and wait for a response. You are seeking a Yes or No answer at this point in the conversation. Be prepared to ask the question more than once if necessary to get to a Yes or No.

Great!

This begins the interview portion of the call. Use this list as a guide to begin asking key questions to fact-find and begin to establish rapport. Keep in mind that every script is meant to be a road map, so feel free to ad-lib and create your own questions in the moment, depending on your prospect's receptiveness.

1. What has you in a position that you are seeking ways to create income from home?

2. What is your current vocation?

3. How long have you been doing that? Is it something you enjoy?

4. Have you ever owned or run your own business or been involved in an entrepreneurial opportunity before? (If yes) What was it? Did you like it? Why not?

5. What exactly would you be looking for in a new business? In other words, what qualities would be important or appealing to you?

6. How long have you been looking for an opportunity?

7. Have you looked at any other businesses? (If yes) Which businesses? Did you get started? Why or why not?)

8. Have you set aside any start-up capital to start your own business this year?

9. Do you consider yourself to be a person who is motivated to earn $1000, $5,000, even $10,000 per month and more, provided you feel good about the right opportunity?

Everybody says Yes to that question, but does everybody mean it?

_____, motivation and action are required to earn that kind of money and reach that level of success. I have found that there are two key components required to create success in our industry: moderate people skills and lots of desire.

Are you in a position to receive information about a great opportunity and – provided you feel good about our company, products, and services – create an educated decision about changing the quality of your present life?

Excellent!

What I am going to do is take you through a very simple two-step process where you can review our products, services, and compensation plan to receive the information you require to determine if there is a fit between your dreams and our opportunity. Do you have a pen?

This is where you let them know where to find your website, online presentation, conference call, or your company's system of presenting information for your prospects. If your company uses meetings to present your opportunity, this is also when you ask them if they can commit to coming to one of your meetings in the next seven business days.

I am seeking people who are serious about changing the quality of their lives and can commit to reviewing this information and reconnecting with me within the next twenty-four to forty-eight hours. Is this you?

Great! Let me give you my number so you can contact me once you have reviewed our presentation _____.

I have an opening for a follow-up appointment on _____ (day) at _____ (time) or on _____ (day) at _____ (time). Which is best for you?

Excellent! I have scheduled you in my calendar for _____ (time) on _____ (day).

My direct number is _____.
Because I value your time as much as mine, I will be available promptly at the time of our appointment. Is this a time you can absolutely commit to being available?

The only answer that qualifies here is an absolute Yes response. If you receive any answer other than Yes, be prepared to re-ask and rephrase the question until you receive it!

Fantastic. Before I let you go, will you please confirm the day and time of our appointment as well as my direct office number?

Perfect. I know you will enjoy the information in our overview. Feel free to contact me before our appointment if you have any questions about getting started, or if you desire any additional information about our company, products, services, and pay plan before our meeting.
Thank you for your time, and YOU create an outstanding day!

Jeffery and Erica Combs: Powerful Prospecting Script

(Can be adapted for newspaper ads, postcards, cold-calling, and warm market)

Hello, may I speak with _____?

Hello, _____. My name is _____ from _____. You recently responded to my advertisement about generating income from the comfort of your home. Is that correct?

Great! The company I represent was founded ___year/years ago for self-explanatory reasons: strength in numbers, security, longevity, and most of all, prosperity for all of our associates. We are one of the leading companies in the exciting _____ industry.

All of my results are created from the comfort of my own home via the telephone. Success in our company requires two traits: moderate people skills and most of all, *a lot* of desire.

Now, let me stress that the type of person I am looking for has a lot of desire. Do you believe you have those two qualities _____? Great! You sound like the type of person I am looking for. Do you have access to a computer? (If prospect says no, ask them if there is a place where they can access a computer) So, if I want to get some information out to you immediately, you can receive it?

In the age of technology, information about a company or service is not sent via mail.

DO NOT MAIL INFORMATION! If your prospect is serious about building a business, they will find a way to receive information via fax, email, Internet, etc.

Great!

This begins the interview portion of the call. Use this list as a guide to begin asking key questions to fact-find and begin to establish rapport. Keep in mind that every script is meant to be a road map, so feel free to ad-lib and create your own questions in the moment, depending on your prospect's receptiveness.

1. What do you do for a living?
2. How long have you been doing that?
3. Are you satisfied with that? (If no, why not?)
4. How much income are you accustomed to?
5. And most importantly, how much income are you looking to generate in the next 12 months?

Great, so you are a big thinker. You sound exactly like the type of person I am looking for.

What I am going to do is take you through a very simple two-step process where you can review our products, services, and compensation plan to receive the information you require to determine if there is a fit between your dreams and our opportunity. Do you have a pen?

This is where you let them know where to find your website, online presentation, conference call, or your company's system of presenting information for your prospects. If your company uses meetings to present your opportunity, this is also when you ask them if they can commit to coming to one of your meetings in the next seven business days.

If you have a live conference call or "sizzle call," follow the script below. Otherwise, refer to the previous script to complete the conversation.

Now _____, here's exactly what I will do: I have _____ (qty) live conference calls on _____ (day) twice a day and one on _____ (day). The purpose of this call is to give you information about our company, products, and services and about how you can generate the kind of income you're looking for. Now, I have two calls tonight at _____ or _____. Which one is best for you? Great. What I will do is call you at_____(five minutes before the hour) and with professional courtesy, I'll expect you to be there. If for any reason you cannot attend, here is my number to call and let me know.

Have a great day and thanks for your time. Good-bye!

YOUR POSTURE WILL DETERMINE YOUR PROSPERITY!

Bringing Prospects to a Presentation Call and Then to the Wrap-Up

Hi, _____, this is _____. How are you feeling? Are you ready for our call?

Great.

You've got your pen and paper and you're in a nice quiet spot?

Terrific.

OK, now I am going to take us into the main presentation call, where we'll be joining about 400 other people from around the country. They'll be starting the call at the top of the hour, and it will last about twenty-five minutes. First they'll talk about the products; then they'll go into the marketing plan and open up the line for questions. Feel free to jump in and ask any questions you have. Then, at the end of the presentation hold on, because I'll still be here, and at that point I'm going to show you how we create the money here! And that is very exciting! OK, great, here we go.

1. Flash to Main Presentation Call.

2. REMEMBER TO:
   • Flash over and make sure you have your guest with you BEFORE you enter the meeting.
   • Introduce you guest on the line: "Hi, this is_____from_____; please welcome my guest _____ from _____. (use FIRST NAMES and STATE)
   • MUTE the line after you introduce your guest.
   • UNMUTE for the questions portion and then mute your phone again after the question period.
3. At the END of the PRESENTATION PORTION of the call, hit your FLASH button and check in with your guest:

Hi, _____, now that you have received information about our products and services, you're going to learn how we qualify and how we create money here. Hold on.

4. Then hit your FLASH button again to connect your prospect back to the call.
* Remember to MUTE your line!

5. Let your team leader walk everyone through how money is created.

6. After the wrap-up: FLASH off the team line and go straight to the three-way!

7. DO NOT ASK PERMISSION to introduce them to members of the team. Just say either: "Hold on" and go get someone to three-way into OR "OK, _____, hang on, and I'll introduce you to some other members of our team." And then go get at least one three-way.

8. FAST, SHORT, TESTIMONIALS. Let the person you three-way in do the talking.
You FLASH to the three-way person. They answer, you say:

Hi _____ (team member), this is _____ (your name). I have _____ (prospect) on the line – can you do a quick three-way?

You can give them a ONE LINE intro to the person, like "Mary is a single mom, and we just came off the live call" (or something to that effect). KEEP IT SHORT!

9. After the three-way call, always ASK for the sale....

On a scale from one to ten, one meaning you have no interest and ten, you can't wait to start creating revenue with us, where would you put yourself on the scale?

If eight or higher:

Great! Does this mean you are ready to get started?

When they say Yes:

Ask them which credit card they'd like to use to get started now!

If seven or lower:

What questions do you have or what information can I provide for you to assist you in deciding that this opportunity is right for you?"

You can also refer to the Neutralizing Objections section for more information to determine where your conversation is going to go at this point!

Now you are finished with that prospect and on to your next one! GOOD JOB!

Neutralizing Objections

The best way to neutralize any objection in a conversation is always to say what you feel and use your prospect's words in the objection in a question of your own to receive clarification about what your prospect really meant. Here are several examples of objections and ways to neutralize them:

Prospect Interrupts You

First, remember to smile and not take this personally. You are about to exercise the ultimate takeaway. Remember that your prospect will ultimately disqualify himself/ herself from collaborating with your team if he/she does not change their modus operandi!

You know, _____, right now I am seeking people I can collaborate with to create a long-term business relationship, and this conversation is not starting on the right note. If you are absolutely serious about generating income from the comfort of your home in order to change the quality of your life, then I have a few simple questions to ask you so I can direct you to the right information for you to determine if this is the right opportunity for you. _____, are you seriously interested in creating wealth from the comfort of your home?

If prospect says Yes:

Great! *(continue your interview)*

If prospect says No:

Before I let you go, can I ask you one last question? I can appreciate that this might not be for you, but do you know any big thinkers like me you would be willing to refer me to who would have an interest in creating an additional stream of income?

Pyramid Objection

First, remember to smile and not take this personally. Anyone asking this question is simply uneducated about your industry!

_____, exactly what do you mean by a "pyramid?"

Now your prospect explains to you what he/she believes a pyramid is.

Is this the kind of opportunity you have been seeking?
Prospect says "NO!"

Great! Because that is absolutely not what we do! Are you in a position to take a closer look at our products, services, and opportunity?

Now continue your interview.

"I Don't Have the Time" Objection

_____, I can appreciate that your life is already complex, but tell me, how does it feel to know you are about to let a great opportunity pass you by?

_____, I can appreciate that your life is hectic, but isn't this why you are looking for a way to create additional income from the comfort of your home?

"I Don't Have the Money" Objection

When you receive this objection, stay powerful in your posture. Most people will give you this objection by reflex, and then actually expect you to believe that they believe they can start a business with no investment required! When they see the value of the opportunity you are representing, they will find the money 99 percent of the time!

_____, I can appreciate your financial position, but do you see an opportunity here for yourself?

_____, I can appreciate that you may not have the money in your bank account today, but if money were not an issue, would you get started today?

_____, if you DID have the money, would you get started today?

_____, are you an expert in creative financing? Are you serious enough about changing the quality of your life to apply your creativity to creating the money to get started?

"This Costs Too Much!" Objection

Easiest response:

What makes you say that? What is the reason?

Insist that your prospect gets specific about what this means.

_____, what are you comparing this investment amount to?

Ask them to consider the value.

_____, price is an important consideration, isn't it? Would you consider value equally important? Do you see the value of our products or opportunity?
_____, what amount were you planning to invest in an opportunity that could change the quality of your life?

If your company offers this option, show them how the investment can be easier to swallow.

_____, would you be ready to get started today if we could translate this investment into installments which are easier to swallow?

"I Need to Think About It" Objection

When you receive this objection, realize that you are talking to an analytical thinker and that this personality type typically will not decide until they have all of the facts, figures, logic, and research and the decision makes complete sense to them. The easiest situation to create here is to direct this person to where he/she can do the research and leave them with your number to call you with questions.

_____, what exactly would you like to think about?
_____, you must have reason for saying that. I would like to know what that is.
_____, you sound like the type of person who wants to read all of the research before creating an intelligent decision. Is this true?

Prospect says Yes.

Great! Do you have a pen? Here is a website where you can research our company, products, and opportunity: www._____.com. My direct number is _____.

Please feel free to contact me with any additional questions you may have when you have reviewed this information and feel good about what you see. Thank you for your time and YOU have a great day!

"How Much Money Have YOU Made?" Objection

When you receive this objection, stay powerful in your posture. This is a "prove it works" question, and if you allow it to intimidate you, the conversation is over. Realize that your results have absolutely nothing to do with the results your prospect may or may not create!

Actually, _____, I am just getting started, but I am directly connected to one of the top income earners in our area. Would you like to meet him/her?
None yet, I just got started. Do you see an opportunity?
_____, that's a great question. Specifically, what would you like to know?
_____, that's a great question. Why do you feel my results have any bearing on the results you could create in this opportunity?
_____, that's a great question. Before I answer it, have you considered what kind of results you would like to create on a monthly basis in this opportunity?

In the sales industry, people are your business regardless of the product or commodity you are representing. It is imperative that you actively prospect to sift and sort through the masses of society to find the few who are ready to collaborate with you. If you have felt stuck in a rut of not knowing what to say or when to say it, many of your excuses for not prospecting have just been neutralized. Ha! Got ya!

Now that you have several simple and powerful tools, it is time for you to get out there and expose other people to your opportunity by using these tools!

It is time to put yourself in the position to take advantage of your ability to create sales opportunities, not just respond to them.

It is time to pick up the phone or leave your home office, get in your car, head to the nearest public gathering place, and connect with people. After all, to capitalize on your selling experience you first require someone to sell to!

So go forth and garner some new and uncharted sales experiences. You deserve to connect with people, and they deserve to connect with you. Most importantly, you deserve a sale!

Tip to Stay on Target:

Today's Date: _____

Time I can realistically prospect:
From:_____   To: _____

New Calls to Create New Connections: _____
Voicemail Messages Left: _____
Quality Conversations: _____
Calls to Referrals: _____
Calls to Existing Clients: _____
(Purpose is generating repeat business or asking for a referral)

Follow-Up Calls: _____
Appointments Created as a Result: _____
Sales Created as a Result:
_____ = $ _____ Profit

PROSPECTING with POWER

Presented by
ERICA COMBS

A Production of
Golden Mastermind Seminars, Inc.

PROSPECTING IS EASY WHEN YOU ARE IN YOUR POWER!

In this signature 8-CD audio program, Erica Combs reveals her secrets to:

- Prospecting With Power
- Prospecting With Posture
- Prospecting for Prosperous Business Partners
- Stepping Into Your Power
- Mastering Your Craft
- Creating Prosperity in Business and in Life

The information in this program is designed to create internal transformations so you can prospect and prosper effortlessly from your power. If you are ready to create financial success, you absolutely deserve to receive the insights Erica shares in *Prospecting With Power*!

www.GoldenMastermind.com

www.WOMENinPOWER.net

I invite you to actively participate with me to create a culture to support entrepreneurial women worldwide. The Women in Power website will provide you with valuable resources and connections created to assist you as you build your enterprise and expand your personal power.

To celebrate the success of entrepreneurial women in free enterprise, I'd like to invite you to share your personal stories with other powerful women. What kind of an impact has Women in Power had on you, and what insights did you gain from your reading? How has what you read made a difference in the way you approach your business?

Contact me directly at www.WomenInPower.net to receive a free gift I have created for you to use each and every day to reaffirm your power to create the peace and self-acceptance you have always desired and absolutely deserve!

Women In Power Unite!

Erica Combs

Erica Combs is the vice president of Golden Mastermind Seminars, Inc. and an internationally recognized speaker, author, and trainer. Her experience in free enterprise combined with her personal growth has allowed her to step into her power and assist her clients to reconnect with their power and brilliance to create quantum changes in their enterprises and in their lives!

Based upon her personal experience, Erica can assure you firsthand that success as an entrepreneur requires an entirely different level of self-esteem, communication, focus and permission than most people are taught is acceptable by their families, coworkers, and peers. Success will require that you begin to examine your current beliefs and give yourself permission to release those which no longer serve you so that you may adopt new and empowering beliefs to lead you to manifesting your dreams.

Erica's coaching and training focuses on creating a foundation for you to begin your journey to personal power, and to create an anchor you can use to reconnect with your internal peace as you continue your journey of personal development in the land of free enterprise.

Erica is available for consulting, mentoring, and personal one-on-one coaching. Her professional guidance will assist you to create maximum results now! Erica doesn't teach theory - she teaches the same skills she uses in business so you can begin creating the results you desire in free enterprise today!

For further information, please call 800-595-6632 or visit her website at www.GoldenMastermind.com.

Golden Mastermind
Seminars, Inc

Vice president of Golden Mastermind Seminars, Inc.

President of More Heart Than Talent Publishing, Inc.

Internationally recognized speaker and trainer

Specializes in self-esteem, leadership, posture, prosperity consciousness, spiritual enlightenment, emotional resilience, and understanding the connection between your emotions and your current circumstances

Has coached and assisted six figure earners and fledgling entrepreneurs from all walks of life

Creator of the transformational Women In Power program & author of *Women In Power: A Woman's Guide to Free Enterprise*

Erica Combs

FREE

"More Heart Than Talent" Teleconference training call with Erica & Jeffery Combs every Tuesday night

Time: 10:30 pm EST
Call: 212-461-5860 / PIN 7707#

800-595-6632
www.GoldenMastermind.com

BREAKTHROUGHS TO SUCCESS

A 2$\frac{1}{2}$ Day Intensive Personal Growth &
Entrepreneurial Retreat Featuring Jeffery & Erica Combs
Location: Stockton, CA

Breakthroughs Exercises:

- The Psychology of Wealth
- Letting Go of Your Ego!
- Emotional Healing
- Getting Money Right Emotionally
- Forgiveness
- Being in the Moment

Breakthroughs To Success will assist you to breakthrough and heal the emotional barriers that have kept you from achieving the level of success you deserve in your enterprise. Spend 2$\frac{1}{2}$ empowering days with Jeffery & Erica Combs in a small, private setting.

Receive luxury transportation to and from the Sacramento airport via limousine service, catered lunches, and hands-on training with Jeff & Erica!

Release Your Limitations & Discover The Power of Belief!

YOU DESERVE TO HAVE IT ALL!

800-595-6632
www.GoldenMastermind.com

NOTES

Notes

Notes

_____
_____
_____
_____
_____
_____
_____
_____
_____
_____
_____
_____
_____
_____
_____
_____
_____
_____
_____
_____
_____
_____
_____
_____
_____

Notes

_____

_____

_____

_____

_____

_____

_____

_____

_____

_____

_____

_____

_____

_____

_____

_____

_____

_____

_____

_____

_____

_____

_____

_____

NOTES

_____

_____

_____

_____

_____

_____

_____

_____

_____

_____

_____

_____

_____

_____

_____

_____

_____

_____

_____

_____

_____

_____

_____

_____

_____

Notes